E-Mail for English Teaching

E-Mail for English Teaching

Bringing the Internet and
Computer Learning Networks
Into the Language Classroom

Mark Warschauer

Teachers of English to Speakers of Other Languages, Inc.

Typeset in ITC Avant Garde and Utopia by
World Composition Services, Inc., Sterling, Virginia
and printed by
Pantagraph Printing, Bloomington, Illinois USA

Helen Kornblum *Director of Communications and Marketing*
Ellen Garshick *Copy Editor*
Ann Kammerer *Cover and art*

Teachers of English to Speakers of Other Languages, Inc.
1600 Cameron Street, Suite 300
Alexandria, VA 22314 USA
Tel 703-836-0774 • Fax 703-836-7864

ISBN 0-939791-62-5
Library of Congress Catalog No. 95-061046

Contents

Acknowledgments

This book is itself an affirmation of its central premise—that the use of electronic communication greatly facilitates collaborative learning and the social production of knowledge.

Space limitations prevent me from listing the scores of people from whom I've gathered ideas and information. I would like to acknowledge at least the following people whose support has been invaluable: Lloyd Holliday, Tom Robb, and Lonnie Turbee of the Student List project; Ruth Vilmi, Linda Mak, Linda Thalman, and Bill Burns of the Email Project; Richard Schmidt, David Ashworth, and David Hiple of the University of Hawai'i; Aniko Balazsik and Roland Vargas of *Wings*; Janice Cook and Judith Kirkpatrick of Kapiolani Community College; and Ron Corio, Greg Younger, David Tillyer, Bruce Roberts, Seppo Tella, Nancy Kroonenberg, Marilyn Martin, Rachel Koch, Candace Chou, H. Douglas Brown, and Keiko Hirata. I also thank Jack Richards and Helen Kornblum of TESOL, as well as three anonymous TESOL publications reviewers, for their support, assistance, and excellent suggestions.

For the dozens of other people whose ideas and inspiration have found their way into this book, I hope I have fairly credited you throughout. If not, I apologize for the oversight and ask that you notify me of my mistake. And it goes without saying that any errors are my sole responsibility.

Mark Warschauer
University of Hawai'i at Manoa
e-mail: *markw@uhunix.uhcc.hawaii.edu*
World Wide Web: *http://www2.hawaii.edu/~markw*

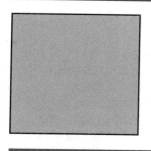

Introduction

Time, Newsweek, and the *New York Times* have all hailed it: The electronic mail (e-mail) revolution is here. In universities, schools, businesses, and homes around the world, millions of people are connecting to each other for instantaneous, inexpensive communication and resource sharing via personal computers.

How does the e-mail revolution apply to English language teaching and learning? Here are just a few of the ways:

- In Hungary, students correspond daily on international discussion lists with students from Norway, the U.S., Canada, Korea, Japan, Australia, and Indonesia. They later decide to jointly publish an international student news magazine called *Wings*.
- ESL students in Eugene, Oregon, submit their dialogue journals by e-mail rather than on paper. The students communicate much more naturally and frequently this way, and the teacher can respond much more quickly and easily.
- A teacher in New York learns she's teaching a class in English pronunciation for Spanish speakers, but she has no experience in this area. She posts a question via e-mail on an English teachers' list, and within 24 hours a half a dozen colleagues around the world have e-mailed her concrete suggestions.

- ESL pupils in a Washington, DC, elementary school find keypals (keyboard pen pals) in several other states and countries. Their attitude toward writing changes dramatically in 2 months.
- A teacher in Japan would like to teach the story "Rip Van Winkle" but doesn't have the text. She finds it from home in 10 minutes using her personal computer and a modem connection to the Internet.
- EFL and ESL university students in Finland, Hong Kong, and the U.S. engage in an international competition to find a solution to a real-world environmental problem. They work in international teams to write technical reports, 3-year plans, and abstracts for an international environmental conference, and then vote on the winning entry and post it electronically for others around the world to see.

WHY USE E-MAIL?

For a busy teacher, learning to use e-mail and the Internet takes a certain amount of effort, and setting up a program for student use takes even more time and effort. Why go to this effort? What are some concrete reasons for using e-mail in the English classroom?

First, e-mail provides students an excellent opportunity for real, natural communication. Many of our students—often even those living or studying in English-speaking countries—lack sufficient opportunities for communicating in English. E-mail can put students in contact with native speakers and/or other English learners across town or around the world in minutes and provide the authentic contexts and motivations for communication that teachers are always trying to supply.

Second, e-mail empowers students for independent learning. The use of e-mail and the Internet involves a whole of range of skills including knowing how to use a personal computer, knowing how to navigate the immense resources of what is often called cyberspace, and becoming familiar with the special register of e-mail communication (which lies somewhere between the formality of traditional writing and the spontaneity of speech). Mastering these skills can empower our students to use e-mail and other types of telecommunication for the rest of their lives, potentially benefiting not only their skills in English but also their personal and professional development in many other ways.

Finally, the use of e-mail enriches our experiences as teachers. E-mail allows us to communicate easily with thousands of colleagues, sharing new ideas, resources, and materials. It can provide the information, contacts, and stimulation that can make our teaching more effective and enjoyable.

This book is designed to provide all the essential information an English teacher needs to begin using e-mail and the Internet as tools for teaching English—or, for Internet veterans, to take a look at new approaches and ideas. It includes ways that teachers can use the Internet for their own research and communication and a myriad of ways that teachers can involve students in using not only e-mail but also new tools like MOOs and the World Wide Web. Throughout, the book highlights pedagogical factors for teachers to consider when bringing students into collaborative groups referred to as computer learning networks.

Chapter 1 explains what e-mail is and how to start using it. It includes a brief history of e-mail, describes various computer networks such as the Internet, and explains what hardware, software, and accounts you need to start using e-mail.

Chapter 2 introduces the ways teachers can use e-mail and the Internet on their own, for collaboration and communication with colleagues and for accessing ESL materials and resources.

Chapter 3 discusses the uses of e-mail and computer networking in a single classroom, including e-mail dialogue journals, writing assignments on e-mail, formal and informal teacher-student consultations via e-mail, and electronic discussion and document sharing.

Chapter 4 discusses the vast possibilities for using e-mail and the Internet for cross-cultural communication, ranging from simple pen pal arrangements to elaborate multicultural research projects and simulations.

Chapter 5 introduces the use of e-mail in distance education to teach language, to provide cultural orientation, and to train teachers.

Chapter 6 discusses ways that teachers and students can gather data, information, and resources from libraries, data bases, and bulletin boards around the world using special tools for the Internet.

Chapter 7 discusses ways of integrating all of the above within an educational program. It looks at the nature of teacher-student and student-student relations in an electronic classroom and examines several models of successful courses that make use of e-mail and computer learning networks.

The book concludes with an extensive bibliography, a list of journals relevant to teachers using e-mail and the Internet, a description of organizations and mailing lists of interest to English teachers and students working with e-mail and the Internet, and a glossary.

The field of telecommunications is expanding at breakneck speed. Undoubtedly many readers will soon come up with—or perhaps have already come up with—many other ways of using e-mail in the classroom. Indeed, e-mail provides so many opportunities for communication, collaboration, and information sharing that rapid innovation is inevitable. So let this book be your guide to getting started, and you and your students may soon be adding your own contributions to the exciting new area of education—and sharing them with us on the Internet!

Getting Started

This chapter explains what e-mail is and how it works, introduces many other forms of electronic communication and research that can take place on local computer networks and on the Internet, and tells you exactly what you need to start using e-mail for English teaching.

THE HISTORY OF E-MAIL

Electronic mail (e-mail) was started in the late 1960s by the U.S. military. Military officials were looking for a way that communications could be carried out in the event of a large-scale nuclear war. They needed a system that would be very decentralized, reliable, and fast in case central institutions were destroyed. They came up with e-mail.

Through the early 1970s, e-mail was limited to the U.S. military, defense contractors, and universities doing defense research. By the 1970s it had begun to spread more broadly within university communities. By the 1980s, academics in a number of fields were using e-mail for professional collaboration. The early 1990s saw an explosion of the use of e-mail and other computer networking tools for a wide range of professional, academic, and personal purposes. Whereas a few thousand people were using e-mail in 1980, it is estimated that more than 25 million people throughout the world were using it in the mid-1990s.

HOW E-MAIL WORKS

E-mail is a way of sending a message from one computer to one or more other computers around the world. First, you write down the e-mail address of the person you're sending the message to. Then you compose the message, either by writing it directly in an special e-mail software program (such as Eudora, Pine, Elm, or MM) or by writing it first in a word-processing program and then transferring (uploading) it into the e-mail software. You push a button to issue a simple command to send the message. The computer system you are connected to will break the message up into tiny pieces and send them electronically to the destination, usually over common telephone lines. The pieces might travel numerous different routes through various other computers on the way. Then, usually within 2–3 minutes, the pieces will all arrive at their destination, where the receiving computer will reassemble them into a legible message. The person receiving the message can then log into his or her computer account at a convenient time and read the mail.

E-MAIL ADDRESSES

To send and receive e-mail, you need to understand some basics about e-mail addresses. A typical e-mail address is *enjack@cityu.edu.hk*—the e-mail address of ESL teacher and author Jack Richards. The part to the left of the @ sign, *enjack*, is called the *userid* (pronounced *user eye dee*) and has been chosen by Jack as his personal handle. The part to the right is called the *domain* and represents the particular computer that receives and delivers Jack's e-mail.

Guess whose e-mail address this is? *president@whitehouse.gov*

AN E-MAIL MESSAGE

E-mail messages usually come in two parts: the heading and the body. The heading includes important information such as whom the message is from, to whom it is sent, who (if anybody) has received a copy (cc), the date, and the subject.

The body is often written in very informal language that falls somewhere between ordinary spoken and formal English. Sometimes the body includes a special signature at the end with the e-mail or snail mail (postal) address of the sender.

Users of e-mail often use special abbreviations and emoticons (also referred to as *smileys*) to communicate their points. Some popular examples are

BTW	by the way
IMHO	in my humble opinion
:-)	a smiling face

<pre>
;-)   a wink
:-(a frown
</pre>

BTW, if you can't make out the above symbols, tilt your head to the left and look again!

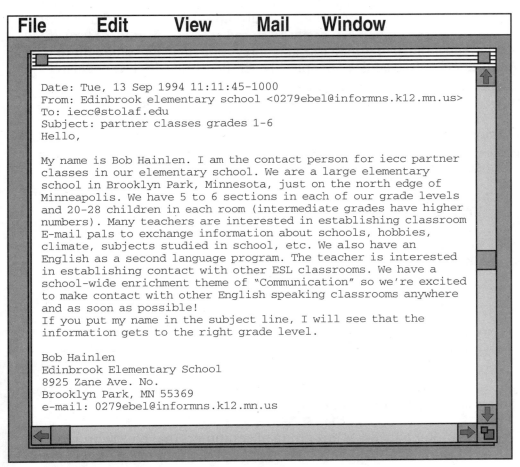

<pre>
 File   Edit   View   Mail   Window

Date: Tue, 13 Sep 1994 11:11:45-1000
From: Edinbrook elementary school <0279ebel@informns.k12.mn.us>
To: iecc@stolaf.edu
Subject: partner classes grades 1-6
Hello,

My name is Bob Hainlen. I am the contact person for iecc partner
classes in our elementary school. We are a large elementary
school in Brooklyn Park, Minnesota, just on the north edge of
Minneapolis. We have 5 to 6 sections in each of our grade levels
and 20-28 children in each room (intermediate grades have higher
numbers). Many teachers are interested in establishing classroom
E-mail pals to exchange information about schools, hobbies,
climate, subjects studied in school, etc. We also have an
English as a second language program. The teacher is interested
in establishing contact with other ESL classrooms. We have a
school-wide enrichment theme of "Communication" so we're excited
to make contact with other English speaking classrooms anywhere
and as soon as possible!
If you put my name in the subject line, I will see that the
information gets to the right grade level.

Bob Hainlen
Edinbrook Elementary School
8925 Zane Ave. No.
Brooklyn Park, MN 55369
e-mail: 0279ebel@informns.k12.mn.us
</pre>

A Typical E-Mail Message

E-MAIL COMPARED WITH OTHER FORMS OF COMMUNICATION

E-mail is both similar to and different from other means of communication (see box). Compared with mail, for example, e-mail is a high-speed method of transferring information that allows rapid exchanges. You can also send large amounts of information by e-mail that would be difficult to communicate by telephone. Unlike the telephone, e-mail allows people to retrieve their messages at any time (although this is possible to a limited extent with answering machines). E-mail allows easier data management than mail, fax, and telephone because all communications and documents arrive via computer and can easily be stored, altered, printed, or forwarded. A major advantage of e-mail is that it allows one message to be sent to hundreds or even thousands of people all over the world very inexpensively.

E-Mail Versus Mail, Fax, and Telephone				
Characteristic	E-Mail	Mail	Fax	Telephone
Transmits at high speed	yes	no	yes	yes
Transmits a large quanity of information	yes	yes	yes	no
Allows easy data management	yes	no	no	no
Allows transmission to one or many	yes	no	no	no
Costs little	yes	?	?	?

E-MAIL AND CYBERSPACE

As powerful as e-mail is, it still represents only one way of communicating by computer. E-mail is one part of the vast international network of computers sometimes referred to as *cyberspace*.

LANs and WANs

A computer network is any group of computers that are electronically linked together. They can be joined by special cable, by ordinary telephone lines, or by satellite.

Computers joined up in one place, such as the English department computer lab, form a local area network (LAN). LANs are usually hard-wired, that is, connected by some sort of cable. When two or more LANs are joined together, via cable or telephone line or satellite, they form a wide area network (WAN). For example, a major university would likely consist of multiple LANs connected into one or more complex WANs. These WANs, in turn, are connected to form even wider WANs. One example of a very large WAN is BITNET, a network of more than 1,000 academic and research organizations in some 40 countries around the world.

The Internet can be referred to as the "mother of all networks." It is a loose collection of LANs and WANs all over the world. Some of these networks are fully integrated into the Internet; others can only exchange certain types of communication with the Internet, such as e-mail. In any case, the Internet represents the largest collection of information and resources ever known to humankind. On the Internet you can

The Internet

- communicate with individuals. More than 25 million people around the world have some kind of connection to the Internet. The most basic way to communicate with individuals is through e-mail, which allows you to send both messages and documents.
- communicate with groups. The Internet allows you to communicate with thousands of people at the same time. Through more than 5,000 e-mail discussion lists on topics ranging from linguistics to Elvis Presley, you can join a community of like-minded individuals for discussion, debate, and exchange. Thousands of newsgroups in the USENET network provide even more flexible and varied ways of communicating with groups. E-mail discussion lists and USENET groups are discussed at length in Chapter 2.
- communicate in real time. E-mail, e-mail discussion lists, and USENET groups all take place *asynchronously*. In other words, the messages take a few minutes to arrive and are later read at the reader's convenience. However, another type of communication is possible on the Internet, called *synchronous* or *real-time* communication.

In real-time communication, the participants (ranging from two to hundreds) must be on-line on different computers at the same time. Whatever one person types immediately appears on the computers of all the other people participating, thus allowing for true electronic discussion to take place. When two people do this, they generally use special software programs called *talk* or *tell*. Discussions among large groups of people often take place through a special service called Internet Relay Chat (IRC).

The most elaborate real-time discussions take place in special simulated environments called *MOOs*. Participants on a MOO can not only speak to the whole group or individuals within the group but can also travel around within a simulated environment and help create that environment. MOOs are becoming very popular for educational purposes, and there is even a special MOO created for ESL students and teachers called *schMOOze University*. Ways of using real-time communication for English teaching and an introduction to schMOOze University are found in Chapters 3 and 4.

■ retrieve information and resources. An incredible array of information resources—including graphics, software, books, library catalogs, bulletin boards, data, sounds, journals, newsletters, newspapers, magazines, and archives—is available via the Internet. The majority of the information is free, though commercial sources are beginning to appear. It takes some time and effort, however, to learn how and where to find this information. Chapters 2 and 6 contain information on what resources are available for English teachers and students and where to begin looking for them.

GETTING STARTED

There are myriad ways to use e-mail and the Internet for English teaching, ranging from the very simple to the quite complicated. For you and/or your students to get started with e-mail, you will need three things: (a) the appropriate hardware, (b) the appropriate software, and (c) e-mail addresses.

You do not need fancy, modern computers to receive and send e-mail. In most cases the most simple models will do. Newer models may have more capabilities for sending or receiving graphics or sound, but you can send basic messages on most any computer. (A complete guide to buying a computer for the first time is beyond the scope of this book. My usual advice is to consider getting the type used by friends or colleagues; their support and help will come in handy.)

Hardware

If you are at a university or large business, your computer may already be hard-wired to other computers in a computer network, which may itself be connected to the Internet. In most cases, however, you will need to connect through the telephone lines to a computer network. To do this, you will need an inexpensive ($50–$300) device called a *modem*.

Modems

Modems can be *external* (an extra piece of equipment that sits on your desk) or *internal* (a card that fits on a slot inside your computer). If you have an Apple Macintosh desktop computer, it's probably better to get an external modem; internal ones may heat up your computer too much. If you have an IBM-compatible (DOS or Windows) desktop computer, you can get either kind (though many people find internal ones more convenient). If you have a notebook computer, it may already come with a modem; if not, for the sake of portability you may want to consider getting a *pocket modem*, which is a small external modem the size of a cigarette pack. The size of the modem does not affect its functioning; you can get a pocket modem for a desktop computer if you so desire.

Modems come at different baud rates that determine the speed at which they can transfer data over telephone lines. (The speed of a modem is also sometimes described as bps, bits per second.) It is generally advisable to spend a little bit more and get a fast modem, at least 14,400 baud (i.e., 14,400 bps), so you will waste less time (and perhaps money, if you are paying for your Internet connection) sending and receiving computer files and documents. In fact, if you can afford it, get a 28,800-baud modem; it's doubtful you'll regret the extra speed.

One more option to consider is a *fax modem*. This device only costs a little bit more than a modem and will allow your computer to send and receive faxes in addition to the basic modem function of connecting you to computer networks.

Finally, the brand of modem does not really make a difference. Buy the best-priced one sold at your local computer store (or by mail order) that has the features (baud rate, size, external/internal, fax/nonfax) you want.

Software

To use a modem, you will need communications software to dial up into a computer network. There are several ways to get communications software. Often it will come free with your modem or bundled with other software on your computer. It also is provided for free with some Internet reference books. Finally, commercial software can be purchased for a relatively cheap price ($50–$250).

Communications software can be confusing to set up, so it is advantageous to try use the software that comes with your modem or computer or, if none is available, to purchase the type used by a friend or colleague who can help you. The following brands are all popular (and I personally recommend the first one listed in each category):

Macintosh: Zterm, VersaTerm, Microphone II, Kermit SmartCom

PC running Microsoft Windows: Procomm Plus for Windows

PC with DOS: Procomm Plus, Qmodem, Kermit

E-Mail Accounts

The last item you will need is one or more e-mail accounts. These accounts will provide you with e-mail addresses and allow you to send and receive messages.

If you are teaching at a university, the computers there may already be hard-wired to a network connected to the Internet. In this case, you will almost certainly be able to receive an e-mail account for free, and it is likely that your students can also.

If you are not at a university, you will likely need some sort of dial-up access to the Internet (making use of a modem and communications software program as discussed above). First ask your school or district computer coordinator. Your school may already have some kind of Internet access, and in many districts teachers can receive e-mail accounts for free. If this is not the case, and you need to make your own arrangements to get access to e-mail and the Internet, you have three basic options: (a) subscribing to an Internet-service provider, (b) subscribing to a commercial on-line service, or (c) finding a local bulletin board system (BBS).

Internet-Service Providers. An internet-service provider will, for a monthly fee, supply you with a dial-up connection to the Internet. This is done in one of two ways: by making your computer act like an Internet *terminal*, or by making your computer an Internet host.

When your computer acts like an Internet terminal, it is not directly on the Internet itself. Rather, it is in communication with a computer, probably a mainframe, that is part of the Internet. You dial a number, make a connection, and perform most important Internet functions, such as sending and receiving e-mail, reading USENET groups, telnetting, and using FTP (described in Chapters 3 and 6).

When your computer becomes an Internet host, it is directly on the Internet itself. This is more complicated (you may need to install some special software called *point to point protocol*—PPP—or *serial line Internet protocol*—SLIP), and your monthly fee will almost certainly be higher. The trade-off is some extra features, such as being able to access (although slowly) graphical and audiovisual material on the World Wide Web (see Chapter 6) and to transfer files from other computers in one direct step rather than two.

For most people the first option is sufficient. In fact, it is the situation of many people who have e-mail accounts from their universities but access them by modem from home.

On-Line Services. On-line services, such as America Online (telephone [800] 827-6364), CompuServe ([800] 374-2002), and Prodigy ([800] 776-3449), offer two advantages over Internet-service providers: (a) They have user-friendly interfaces and (b) they offer their own special data bases, discussion groups, and other resources not accessible via the Internet. However, they also have a disadvantage: They provide incomplete access to the Internet. They usually fail to offer most of the Internet tools (described in Chapter 6), and they sometimes charge a supplemental fee per message for sending and receiving e-mail via the Internet. Even if the fee per message is very small, the cost can add up if you participate in various educational projects.

In addition to the "big three" on-line services mentioned above, two on-line services (owned by the same company) offer complete Internet access: DELPHI ([800] 695-4005) and BIX ([800] 695-4775).

Bulletin Board Systems. The last possibility is to make use of a local BBS.

A BBS functions as a repository of messages and files, often devoted to a single topic. In some cases access a BBS is free; in other cases there is a small monthly fee. Sometimes a BBS provides some limited access to the Internet as one of its services.

There are several problems with attempting to rely on BBSs for Internet access. They are generally very small scale, run by a few people or even an individual. They often have an insufficient number of telephone lines for calling in and connecting. If they do offer Internet service, it will likely be only for a small subset of Internet features.

Making Your Choice

How do you choose a means of Internet access? The first point, as indicated above, is to request and push for your school district or university to provide Internet access. Internet access for teachers or students is seldom granted without a demand. Present a concrete plan to your administration of what you would like to do, based on information in this book and discussion with other people, and you will likely have a better chance of succeeding.

If you do need to pay for service, check newspaper advertisements and computer stores to get the telephone numbers of some Internet-service providers in your local area. Call them and some of the commercial on-line services, and make some comparisons based on your own needs. Here are some factors to consider:

- *e-mail:* Is there a fee for sending e-mail to and receiving e-mail from the Internet? Is e-mail delivered immediately when it comes, or batched together and sent only a few times a day?
- *features:* Does the system include telnet? File Transfer Protocol (FTP)? USENET? Gopher server? World Wide Web server? Archie server? IRC? Any kind of on-line help?
- *cost:* How much is the monthly fee? How many hours of use do you get? Are the times restricted (i.e., just weekends and evenings)? How much will it cost per hour for additional hours of use? Do you gain access with a local or 800 number, or will you need to pay toll or long-distance charges to dial up? (These can really add up!) Is there a free trial membership?

If you are connected to the Internet via a university or an Internet-service provider, you may be offered a choice of program to use for sending and receiving e-mail. Some of the most popular are Eudora, Pine, Elm, MM, and Mail. Eudora and Pine are generally considered the easiest to use, followed by Elm. If you are not given a choice, don't worry about it; all of the programs can do the job, and your system may have its own special e-mail program that you're not aware of. In any case, whichever program you use, you will still be able to communicate with people who use different programs.

Finally, if you are connected to the Internet via a university or a Internet-service provider, your account will be maintained on a centralized, powerful computer. Such computers run on a variety of operating systems (the way personal computers run on operating systems such as DOS, Windows, or Apple OS). The most common of the operating systems for mainframe computers, especially at universities, is called *UNIX*.

Under UNIX, all documents and files are stored in directories and subdirectories that are much like the directories and subdirectories in DOS and Windows and similar to the folders on a Macintosh. If you are working on e-mail, most of what the operating system does will be invisible to you (and you don't really need to know about it to get started). However, as you become a more experienced user, knowing a bit about UNIX will be extremely helpful for sorting, saving, and downloading or uploading files. *Downloading* refers to copying a document or file from your e-mail directory to your personal computer for easier permanent access. Likewise, you can upload files from your word-processing program into your e-mail directory. For instructions, consult your communications software manual or speak with people who are using the same system. Uploading and downloading can save you many hours and bring much added convenience to your use of e-mail.

Depending on your system, you may never need to know anything about the UNIX commands listed below. If you do need the information later, you'll probably find the chart handy.

The following are the most important commands:

Basic UNIX Commands

A. Directory Commands

ls	display a directory listing
cd directory	change to specified directory
cd ..	change to parent directory (one directory up)
pwd	display name of current directory
mkdir directory	make a subdirectory
rmdir directory	delete a subdirectory

B. File Commands

rm file	delete a file
cp file1 file2	copy a file and give the copy a new name
mv file directory	move a file to a new directory
mv file1 file2	rename a file (keeping it in the same directory)
tprint file	print a file on the attached printer

C. Other Commands

man command	display information about that command
passwd	change login password
^c	suspend a command or quit reading a file
logout	exit the UNIX system

One final note: UNIX is case sensitive. Therefore, while using UNIX you must be consistent with your use of capital and lowercase letters. E-mail addresses, though, are almost never case sensitive, so you can relax about the use of capital and lowercase letters in e-mail.

2 E-Mail for Teacher Collaboration

This chapter explains how to use e-mail to collaborate with other teachers and to get information, resources, and materials that will help you teach. It introduces you to TESL-L, a special e-mail discussion list for English teachers, as well as other important discussion lists, newsgroups, and electronic gathering places for language-teaching professionals on the Internet.

The easiest, fastest, and most direct way you can use e-mail is as a tool for your own research, material gathering, and collaboration. All you need is a single computer—at your home, place of work, or school—that has access to the Internet. This one computer can quickly and easily put you in touch with thousands of other ESL teachers around the world as well as with an incredible bank of ESL materials, lesson plans, and even special ESL computer software.

The place to start is an absolutely fabulous resource called TESL-L. Joining TESL-L is almost like having access to the people, material, and resources of a huge teachers' convention from the privacy of your own home or office.

TESL-L

TESL-L was founded in 1991 with the goal of providing educators a fast, convenient, and topical electronic discussion forum that focuses on issues related to teaching ESL/EFL. In 1992 it received a grant from the U.S. Department of Education, Fund for the Improvement of Post-Secondary Education (FIPSE), which has helped it grow faster.

TESL-L is run by three people, Anthea Tillyer of the City University of New York, Susan Simon of the City University of New York, and Tom Robb of Kyoto-Sangyo University in Japan. Dozens of other volunteers and thousands of participating teachers have helped to make TESL-L a great success and invaluable resource. More than 4,000 teachers in 70 countries are members of TESL-L, making it one of the largest e-mail discussion forums in the world. TESL-L founder Tillyer received a special commendation at the 28th Annual TESOL Convention in 1994 for the great service that TESL-L has rendered to the ESL/EFL world community.

What You Can Do on TESL-L

Imagine you're teaching a course for the first time, and you're not sure which book to use for that particular course and level. Or perhaps you have questions about the advantages or disadvantages of a particular approach, method, or technique or about a particular type of language learner. Or you want to inquire about employment conditions in a particular country or about a new (or old) theory of second language acquisition.

On TESL-L, you can ask questions about these or any other related topics of several thousand teachers around the world—and probably within 24 hours 5 or 10 will have offered you specific suggestions or comments. You can do much more than ask questions; you can share your own ideas and experiences and actively collaborate with your colleagues around the world to collectively develop new answers to all types of questions.

How TESL-L Works

TESL-L is an e-mail discussion list, sometimes referred to as an e-mail mailing list. TESL-L and other such lists are also often called *LISTSERVs*, named after the special LISTSERV software program that runs many of them.

TESL-L and other e-mail mailing lists work much the same way as a traditional mailing list run by a church, office, or professional organization. The thousands of TESL-L members have their names and e-mail addresses encoded in a computerized mailing list so that e-mail messages can be sent out to all of them. Consider the advantages of such a list compared with a traditional snail mail (postal service) mailing list:

- *simplicity:* Messages are sent out to all the members of the list with the click of a single button, rather than by laboriously stuffing and

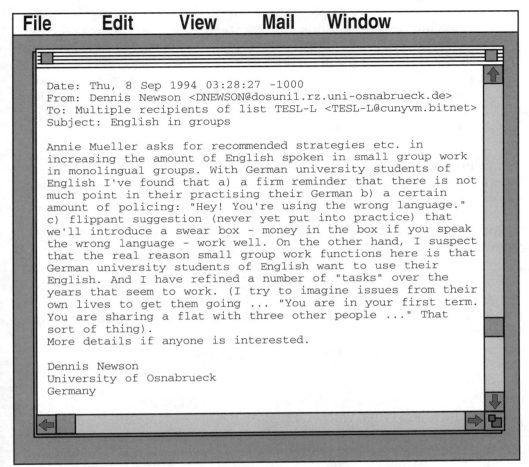

```
File        Edit        View        Mail        Window
```

```
Date: Thu, 8 Sep 1994 03:28:27 -1000
From: Dennis Newson <DNEWSON@dosuni1.rz.uni-osnabrueck.de>
To: Multiple recipients of list TESL-L <TESL-L@cunyvm.bitnet>
Subject: English in groups

Annie Mueller asks for recommended strategies etc. in
increasing the amount of English spoken in small group work
in monolingual groups. With German university students of
English I've found that a) a firm reminder that there is not
much point in their practising their German b) a certain
amount of policing: "Hey! You're using the wrong language."
c) flippant suggestion (never yet put into practice) that
we'll introduce a swear box - money in the box if you speak
the wrong language - work well. On the other hand, I suspect
that the real reason small group work functions here is that
German university students of English want to use their
English. And I have refined a number of "tasks" over the
years that seem to work. (I try to imagine issues from their
own lives to get them going ... "You are in your first term.
You are sharing a flat with three other people ..." That
sort of thing).
More details if anyone is interested.


Dennis Newson
University of Osnabrueck
Germany
```

A Typical Message on TESL-L

    mailing thousands of envelopes.

- ■ *speed:* Whether traveling a few doors down or halfway around the world, the messages arrive within a matter of minutes rather than taking days or even weeks.
- ■ *cost:* The messages are almost always sent virtually free, as most universities already have agreements allowing them unlimited academic

use of the Internet. (A program as large as TESL-L does involve considerable costs for administration, which in this case are covered by the FIPSE grant, by support from the City University of New York, and by many dedicated volunteers.)

■   *accessibility:* The thousands of list members have access to the mailing list and can use it to generate their own message to the entire list; what's more, any member can quickly or easily reply either to the individual or to the entire list.

It is no wonder that TESL-L and other LISTSERV mailing lists have become enormously popular with academic, professional, and social organizations in recent years.

Joining TESL-L

Joining TESL-L, or any other LISTSERV mailing list, is very easy. In the case of TESL-L, send an e-mail message to the following address:

listserv@cunyvm.cuny.edu

(If your e-mail address ends in *bitnet,* send your message to *listserv@cunyvm.bitnet*) In your message, leave the subject line blank. In the body of your message, write

sub TESL-L yourfirstname yourlastname
(for example, *sub TESL-L Jane Doe*)

Your subscription to TESL-L will be automatically registered.

One final point: When you send the sub message to LISTSERV, you are communicating with a computer, not with a human being. Therefore there is nothing to be gained by trying to add explanatory remarks, and you may end up canceling or distorting your intended action.

The Welcome Message

After you join TESL-L, you will be sent a very detailed welcome message by e-mail. Welcome messages are a standard part of LISTSERV mailing lists and should be read carefully. In the case of the TESL-L welcome message, it is probably a good idea to both print it out and download it for further reference.

The TESL-L welcome message will bring you the following information:

- how to read and reply to TESL-L messages
- how to send your own messages to TESL-L
- how to get access to the extensive TESL-L archives (see below)
- how to join one of the many TESL-L sub-branches (see below)
- how to get on-line help if you're having problems with any aspect of using TESL-L

Keep your welcome message in a handy place. You'll probably refer to it often.

If you're like most new discussion list members, you'll want to lurk awhile when you first join the discussion. *Lurking* in cyberspace refers to quietly reading other people's postings (messages) without immediately jumping into the discussion. It's not considered bad manners at all and is actually very good netiquette (net etiquette—see below) because it allows you to get a feel for the discussion before plunging in.

Soon you will probably have the very human urge to jump into the discussion. To do this, you will post (send) your first message. As the TESL-L welcome message says, "To read is fine, but to post is divine!"

How do you post a message to TESL-L? The first and perhaps most important thing to note is the *difference between the list address and the LISTSERV address.* The LISTSERV address for TESL-L is *listserv@cunyvm.cuny.edu* (or *listserv@cunyvm.bitnet* for BITNET users). You use this address to send commands to the computer (*subscribe, set nomail*, etc.) However, if you want to post a message, you must write directly to the list and not to the LISTSERV computer program. Send your message to

> *TESL-L@cunyvm.cuny.edu*
> (or *TESL-L@cunyvm.bitnet*)

The distinction between sending commands to the computer and posting a message is very important to keep in mind. It applies not just to TESL-L but to all e-mail discussion groups. If you post your opinions about grammar teaching, for example, to the LISTSERV (*listserv@...*) rather than to the list (*TESL-L@...*), they will be read only by a computer! And if you send your "housekeeping command" (e.g., *set xxx nomail*) to the list (*TESL-L*) rather than to the LISTSERV (*listserv@...*), it will be read by several thousand teachers around the world!

When posting to TESL-L or any e-mail discussion list, keep in mind several points of good e-mail manners, or netiquette. First, keep your message relatively short and to the point, as many subscribers have to process dozens of messages a day (and some even have to pay for their e-mail, line for line). TESL-L has a strictly enforced limit of 50 lines (two screens). Second, write a clear, brief description of the content of your message on the subject line so people can judge whether or not to read your message.

Finally, go out of your way to be polite and courteous. E-mail, which involves faceless, instantaneous communication among thousands of different people around the world, encourages a rapid, free, but faceless exchange of ideas. Such an exchange can cause misunderstandings and even *flaming* (name-calling or the sending of hostile messages). Many e-mail discussion lists have become very unpleasant as a result of too-frequent bickering and arguing. TESL-L is known as one of the most pleasant and friendly discussion lists around. Help keep it that way by being upbeat and polite in your postings.

Each discussion list develops its own particular netiquette. More details about rules and guidelines are usually contained in the welcome message, which is one more reason to read it carefully and keep it close at hand.

Special Options

The volume of messages sent every day through TESL-L is quite extensive—usually 10–20 messages per day and sometimes more than 30. Therefore you may decide at certain times to set your subscription to a special option to reduce the flow of mail. TESL-L allows you to opt to get an index of the mail (rather than all the individual messages) or even to temporarily stop the mail from coming.

These steps are very easy. In either case, you need to address a message to one of the two TESL-L LISTSERV addresses (use the same address you used for subscribing). Leave the subject line blank. If you prefer to receive only an index of each day's TESL-L mail, send the message

set TESL-L index

If you prefer to stop the mail altogether at least temporarily, send the message

set TESL-L nomail

This command says to the LISTSERV computer, "I want to remain a member of TESL-L (and have continued access to its archives and sublists, and even be able to post a message if I want), but until further notice I want to stop receiving TESL-L mail."

You can reverse either of the two commands (*set TESL-L index* or *set TESL-L nomail*) in the same way: Send an e-mail to the TESL-L LISTSERV address with the message

set TESL-L mail

Many ESL and EFL teachers have special interests that they would like to discuss in addition to, or instead of, discussing more general topics. For this reason, special TESL-L branches have been set up:

TESL-L Branches

TESLCA-L	computer-assisted language learning
TESLFF-L	"fluency first" and whole language pedagogy
TESLIE-L	intensive English programs, teaching and administration
TESLIT-L	adult education and literacy
TESLJB-L	jobs, employment, and working conditions in TESL/TEFL
TESLMW-L	material writers
TESP-L	teachers of English for specific purposes

To join any of these sub-branches, you must first become a member of TESL-L and then send an e-mail to the TESL-L LISTSERV with the message *sub xxx-L yourfirstname yourlastname* (where *xxx-L* represents the name of the list you want to join). For example,

sub TESLJB-L John Doe

(Note the following exception: Subscribers to TESP-L should send their subscription request to *listserv@listserv.net*, not to the TESL-L LISTSERV address.)

If you decide to participate only in a sub-branch, you can set the main branch (TESL-L) to *nomail* per the instructions above. If you belong to more than one of the TESL-L lists and you want to shut them all down for a while (for example, while taking a vacation), you can set them all to *nomail* by sending the command *set * nomail*. After your holiday, you can start receiving mail from all of them again by sending the message *set * mail*. Further information on the sub-branches and how to join them is included in the TESL-L welcome message.

TESLK-12

Because the use of e-mail started in the academic community and only later trickled down to public schools, many of the members of TESL-L are teachers in colleges and universities. For this reason, a sister discussion list called TESLK-12 was started in January 1994. The goal of TESLK-12 is to facilitate discussion and electronic sharing among teachers of English to children. Unlike the other lists described above, TESLK-12 is not a sub-branch of TESL-L but a separate list with its own separate subscriptions. To join TESLK-12, send a message to

listserv@cunyvm.cuny.edu

In the body of the message, write

sub TESL-K12 yourfirstname yourlastname

TESL-L ARCHIVES

Almost as valuable as the TESL-L discussion list is the TESL-L archives. They include a vast array of files and documents related to English teaching contributed by TESL-L members around the world. TESL-L maintains archives on the following topics:

- classroom practices and activities, for example, FAIRY TALES, FILM COURSE, and LARGE CLASSES
- testing and evaluation, for example, ORALSKIL TESTING, PORTFOLI ASSESSMN, and STUDENT BIAS
- computers in ESL—activities, for example, COMPUTER JOURNLSM, EMAIL PROJECTS, and GLOBAL CLSSROOM
- computer hardware and software, for example, CDROM FILE, SPEECH ANALYSIS, and LANGUAGE LABS
- books, periodicals, and other materials, for example, BOOKS NOVELS, COMPUTER BOOKREV1, and BOOKS DICTNRY

- net resources and e-mail, for example, INTERNET TOPTEN, LISTSERV GUIDE1, and DATABASE SEARCH
- organizations and conferences, including the complete program books of major conferences (TESOL, International Association of Teachers of English as a Foreign Language) several weeks before the conferences
- English learners, countries, and teacher education, for example, PROFILE JAPAN, TEACHING CHINA, and SCHOOL CALENDAR (academic calendars all over the world)
- the English language, for example, ARTICLES FILE and ENGLISH HOMOPHON
- commercial, for example, ONLINE BOOKSTOR and BOOKS TESOL

In addition to these materials, the archives include copies of all the postings to TESL-L over the past few years, archived weekly.

This amazing array of materials is easily retrievable with a few keystrokes from your home or office computer. Once you are a member of TESL-L, you can send an e-mail to one of the two TESL-L LISTSERV addresses (use the same one you used for subscribing). In the body of your message, write

index TESL-L

Within a few minutes, you will automatically be sent a lengthy index listing and describing the hundreds of documents in the TESL-L archives. Once you've selected one you want, send another e-mail to the TESL-L LISTSERV with the message

get xxx xxx TESL-L F=mail

For example, if you would like to get the TESL-L file on ideas for using e-mail with ESL/EFL students (listed in the index as *EMAIL PROJECTS*), send the TESL-L LISTSERV the following message:

get email projects TESL-L F=mail

You can also contribute your own materials to the archives, sharing your ideas and resources with teachers all around the world. Information on how to do so is included in the TESL-L welcome message.

OTHER ELECTRONIC MAILING LISTS

As extensive as TESL-L is, it is only one of many electronic mailing lists that may be of interest to ESL/EFL teachers. Some additional lists are

- LINGUIST: for discussion of language and linguistics (*listserv@tamvm1.tamu.edu*)
- SLART-L: second language acquisition, research, and teaching (*listserv@cunyvm.cuny.edu*)
- MULTI-L: language and education in multilingual settings (*listserv@vm.lbiu.ac.il*)
- LTEST-L: language-testing research and practice (*ltest-l@psuvm.psu.edu*)
- LLTI: language-learning technology international/discussion of computer-assisted language learning (*listserv@dartcms1.dartmouth.edu*)
- FLTEACH: foreign language teaching forum for high school and college teachers (*listserv@ubvm.cc.buffalo.edu*)
- MBU-L: the list of MegaByte University, for discussing issues related to computers and composition (*listproc@unicorn.acs.ttu.edu*)
- EST-L: for discussing issues related to the teaching of English for science and technology (*listserv@asuvm.inre.asu.edu*)
- INCLASS: initiated by the Canadian SchoolNet project, for discussion of using the Internet in the classroom (*listproc@schoolnet.carleton.ca*)
- UK-SCHOOLS: for discussion on using the Internet in U.K. schools (*mailbase@mailbase.ac.uk*)

You can subscribe to all of these lists by sending a basic *sub* message (*subscribe nameoflist yourfirstname yourlastname*) to the indicated e-mail address.

The lists described above are only the tip of the iceberg. An up-to-date 15-page list of e-mail discussion lists on a wide range of topics related to education, languages, and culture is stored in the TESL-L archives; its name is LIST OFLISTS1, and it is accessible to all TESL-L members. After joining TESL-L, send a message to the TESL-L LISTSERV with the message

get list oflists1 TESL-L F=mail

Finally, you can order the entire list of more than 5,000 LISTSERV mailing lists or sections of the list that correspond to your particular specifications. If you would like to order the entire LISTSERV list, send the message *list global to listserv@cunyvm.cuny.edu* (or, if you have a BITNET address, to *listserv@cunyvm.bitnet*). To get a more selective listing, for example, of all lists related to poetry, send the message *list global/poetry* to the same address.

Another valuable resource for ESL/EFL teachers is *USENET newsgroups* (sometimes also called *NETWORK News*). USENET newsgroups are similar to LISTSERV mailing lists in that they allow easy, fast, and inexpensive sharing of resources and ideas among thousands of people all over the world. However, they differ in several important ways.

With LISTSERV mailing lists, all the posted messages are sent into your e-mail mailbox daily. All you have to do is open your mailbox, and you will find messages from TESL-L or any other LISTSERV list you subscribe to.

In contrast, USENET newsgroups are not offered to individual subscribers. Instead, computing centers around the world subscribe to various newsgroups, and individual users use special programs to browse through the groups whenever they're interested. (USENET also contrasts with bulletin board systems [BBSs], which similarly serve as repositories for messages and files but usually hold their files on a single computer rather than making them available to computing centers all over the world.)

Altogether there are more than 5,000 USENET newsgroups, with dozens more being formed every month. The newsgroups cover an incredible array of topics, ranging from particular sexual fetishes to discussion of major international issues. Most universities subscribe and provide access to virtually all the serious newsgroups, including a number related to teaching and learning English and other languages.

There are several different software programs, called *newsreaders*, for accessing USENET newsgroups. The four most common newsreaders are named *tin, rn, trn,* and *nn*. The first thing to determine is whether your computer system provides access to USENET and, if so, via which newsreader. If you have a choice of different newsreaders, you may want to use *tin*, since it is the most recently developed and the one that allows you to scan through a large number of articles and newsgroups most quickly and conveniently.

If you cannot find out whether your system has access to USENET, try typing *tin* at the system prompt and pressing <return>. If nothing happens, type any of the other three commands (*rn, nn, or trn*), press <return>, and see if this produces results.

Newsreaders are easy and straightforward to operate, and all the commands are always available on screen. If you successfully enter the newsreader, type *h* (and press <return>) or *?* (and press <return>) and you will see a complete menu of commands for moving among the groups and reading the news.

Differences Between LISTSERVs and USENET

As mentioned above, one of the differences between LISTSERVs and USENET is who subscribes—the individual or the computer center. The practical effect of this difference is that, unlike with LISTSERVs, USENET messages are not sent to your mailbox. You have to go into USENET at your own convenience and look for what you want. This feature provides both advantages and disadvantages. On the one hand, it can be more work to go into USENET and read messages rather than to have them sent to you. On the other hand, you have the easy flexibility to check out whatever newsgroups you want without having to formally subscribe (and possibly receive lots of daily mail).

Another difference is how the discussions are organized. On LISTSERV mailing lists, the mail comes into your mailbox piece by piece in the order it is sent. With USENET, the discussions are usually *threaded*, with responses to particular comments listed in order by topic.

USENET Groups of Interest to ESL Teachers

TESL-L itself is accessible via USENET for those who cannot or do not want to subscribe to it directly. The name of the group to look for is *bit.listserv.TESL-L.* (However, only members can post contributions, use the archives, or join TESL-L branches.)

According to Jeff Williamson of Northern Virginia Community College, the newsgroup alt.folklore.urban is a great place to let ESL students explore: It is "full of fun stories and maybe good lessons if you're into critical thinking" (posting on TESLCA-L, February 22, 1995).

Other USENET groups of possible interest to ESL or EFL teachers include

- alt.usage.english
- alt.education.email-project
- alt.education.disabled
- alt.education.research
- sci.lang
- soc.culture ... (a large number of newsgroups dealing with dozens of countries and cultures from Afghanistan to Yugoslavia)
- K12 ... (a number of newsgroups dealing with K–12 educational issues and exchanges)

Many other resources are available on USENET, including newsgroups on a wide variety of cultural and social topics. The newsreading software programs (*tin, trn, rn,* and *nn*) each have commands for either browsing through the groups or searching for particular words. In 30 minutes to an hour you can quickly browse through several thousand groups and select any that you find of special interest.

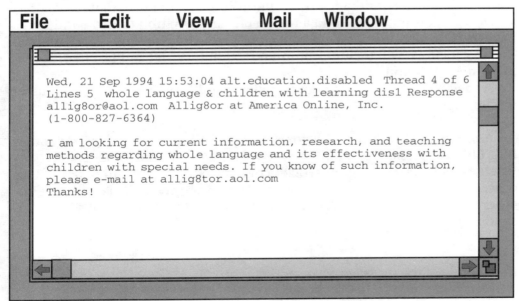

A Sample USENET Message (From alt.education.disabled)

REAL-TIME TEACHER TALK ON MEDIAMOO

LISTSERVs and USENET newsgroups provide a great way to communicate and collaborate with other teachers or language professionals. However, all communication through LISTSERVs or USENET is asynchronous. If you want to have a chance to chat with other teachers on real time, try MediaMOO.

MediaMOO is one of dozens of MOOs set up to provide a place for real-time, live communication among like-minded people. (MOO stands for *multiple-user domain object oriented*, which is unfortunately typical of the confusing jargon on the Internet!) Once you get into a MOO, everything you and other participants type will go right onto everybody else's screen immediately.

Conversations are held on MediaMOO throughout the week on various topics related to education, languages, computers, and communication. One highlight of MediaMOO is Netoric Cafe, a special collective conversation that takes place every Tuesday at 8:00 p.m. U.S. eastern (New York) time on various topics related to education and computer-mediated communication. For detailed instructions on how to participate in MediaMOO and Netoric Cafe, send a request for information to Tari Fanderclai (*tlfand01@homer.louisville.edu*) or to Greg Siering (*00gjsiering@bsuvc.bsu.edu*). The instructions will include commands such as *telnet* and *Gopher*, explained in Chapter 5.

A special MOO for ESL students, called *schMOOze University*, is discussed in Chapter 4.

TESL-EJ, AN ELECTRONIC JOURNAL FOR ESL TEACHERS

Another electronic resource for sharing information and ideas with other ESL/EFL teachers is *TESL-EJ*, a refereed electronic journal for ESL/EFL teachers with a wide range of articles covering both theory and practice. Like other electronic journals, *TESL-EJ* is sent out over e-mail and is available in other electronic formats. Subscriptions to *TESL-EJ* are free. To subscribe, send a message to

listserv@cmsa.berkeley.edu

In the body of the message, write

sub TESLEJ-L yourfirstname yourlastname

For example,

sub TESLEJ-L Jane Doe

Submit full-length articles and general correspondence to Maggi Sokolik, Editor, at *msokolik@uclink.berkeley.edu.*

Another way to read all the articles in TESL-EJ without subscribing, as well as to access lots of other interesting information for English teachers, is by accessing the special TESL/TEFL Gopher files (see Chapter 6).

3

E-Mail in a Single Classroom

This chapter explains ways to use e-mail and other forms of computer networking in a single classroom, the advantages of these activities, and some guidelines for successfully carrying them out.

Many ESL teachers understand why to use e-mail and electronic communication for long-distance communication. After all, they can put English learners together with native speakers of English, or other English-language students, from across the city or across the world. What many teachers don't realize is that e-mail and electronic communication can be of great benefit not only for long-distance exchanges but also for linking the students in a single class. Three types of electronic communication are possible within a single class: teacher-student communication, out-of-class electronic discussion, and in-class, real-time electronic discussion.

TEACHER-STUDENT COMMUNICATION

E-mail for teacher-student communication would most likely take place in higher education, where students might have some independent access to e-mail out of class. In some situations, it might occur at the high school level as well.

Teacher-student communication via e-mail can take several forms, including formal and informal consultation, exchange of dialogue journals, and writing conferencing.

For a student to consult a teacher or professor can be a difficult or even intimidating experience. Many students do not take advantage of teachers' office hours because of shyness, lack of confidence in English, or simply lack of time.

Giving your students your e-mail address and letting them know that questions and comments are welcome is one way of giving them more power to express themselves and communicate with you. If students have access to e-mail at their home or campus computer lab, they can tell or ask you what they want, when they want, without having to interrupt your privacy with a telephone call or give you a written message that you may not see for days. Providing your students with your e-mail address is thus a way of "leveling the playing field" and overcoming the language and status difficulties ESL students often have in communicating with their teachers.

A busy adjunct teacher at the City University of New York started conducting informal office hours by e-mail a couple of years ago. He finds that his students not only consult him much more frequently but are much more open and communicative in their contacts (Tillyer, 1993).

A very popular technique for fostering student reflection and writing practice is the teacher-student dialogue journal. Students turn in a weekly diary to teachers, who respond to each one with comments, questions, and answers.

Dialogue journals are no doubt effective. But any teacher who has used them can testify to an inherent problem that weakens their effectiveness: the disruptive nature of the collection cycle, with all students turning the journals in on one day and waiting anywhere from a day to a week for the teacher to read them, write on them, and return them.

An alternative that maintains all the benefits of dialogue journals and overcomes this handicap is the electronic dialogue journal. The students submit their dialogue journal by e-mail, and the teacher responds in the same manner. A student can thus receive a response within a day or possibly even less—and we all know that rapid response is a great motivator! As for teachers, they can more easily stagger the collection of journals, receiving them not only on one particular day of class but any time during the week, thus spreading out the work more evenly (and avoiding handling all that paper, the bane of any teacher's existence!).

Wang (1993) of the University of Oregon at Eugene did an extensive study comparing the discourse of ESL students' dialogue journals written in both e-mail and traditional paper format. She found that the students using e-mail journals wrote greater amounts of text, asked more questions, and used different language functions more frequently than did students writing on paper.

These last points are especially important because ESL students often have difficulty expressing their ideas in writing. Using e-mail rather than paper for communication seems to create two advantages: (a) because the communication is going directly and rapidly to the reader, e-mail provides a wonderful sense of audience; and (b) because the words are electronic and are never committed to paper, e-mail seems to allow students to take more risks and to avoid getting terrified of committing original thought to paper.

Teacher-Student Writing Conferencing

The two benefits mentioned for e-mail dialogue journals make e-mail a good tool not only for exchanging those journals but for more general types of writing conferencing between teachers and students.

Modern theories of composition instruction emphasize the importance of developing writing as a process, not just as the creation of a product. The pedagogical emphasis is thus on having students write multiple drafts and on having the teacher play the role of an interested reader rather than a judge or inquisitor.

Yet the fact that compositions have to be printed out, turned in on certain dates, and then handed back places a limit on the natural give-and-take that often takes place in more authentic forms of academic writing. Many teachers of composition, both to native-speaking students and to students learning English, find that students are more willing to submit multiple drafts and to make serious, global revisions when their work is submitted electronically rather than on paper. E-mail provides a perfect mechanism for students to submit drafts and for teachers to look them over at their convenience and send them back with comments—one time, two times, or several times. New ideas are shared when they are fresh and can be responded to quickly. Another advantage is that the teacher can easily store all drafts of a document for later review and analysis of the revision process.

In summary, using e-mail for teacher-student communication can give students more access to their teachers, provide a more convenient channel for sharing student (and teacher) writings, and assist students in developing a better sense of the writing process.

Another way to use e-mail in a single classroom is for out-of-class electronic discussion. Like e-mail for teacher-student communication, electronic discussion can be set up wherever students have regular access to e-mail, for example at a college or university computing center.

The two most common ways to organize out-of-class electronic discussion are with mailing lists or USENET newsgroups.

The simplest way to hold out-of-class electronic discussions is with a class mailing list. The principle behind a class mailing list is exactly the same as that of the LISTSERV lists discussed in Chapter 2. For example, if you are teaching an ESL 101 class, you can create a class mailing list called ESL101-L (mailing lists usually end with *L*, which stands for *list*). Then, when you or any of your students addresses an e-mail message to ESL101-L, it will automatically be sent on to all the members of the list (in this case, the members of the class).

The ways to create a class mailing list boil down to two: create the list yourself or ask your school's computer center staff to do it for you.

Creating a List. The easier way to create a list is to explain to your school's computer center staff that you would like to set up an e-mail discussion list for your class. If you are working at a college or university, the staff will probably be able to set up such a list for you. If the staff is hesitant, explain the many advantages of using e-mail for English teaching and the reasons you want to set up the list. You may be breaking important ground for others at your school to follow.

Once the list is set up, the e-mail addresses of the students will have to be entered in as members. Because the list will probably not be a true LISTSERV, you or someone at the computer center will probably need to type the addresses into the computer rather than having students send them in individually as subscribers. The computer center staff will provide instructions on how to do this.

If the staff is unable or unwilling to set up a class list for you, there is generally a low-tech way to do it yourself. Most e-mail software programs, such as Pine and Elm, include a mechanism for establishing a group alias. In your own e-mail system, you can set up a group alias called, for example, *goodfriends*, with the names and e-mail addresses of your five (or any number of) best friends. Any e-mail you send to *goodfriends* will automatically be sent on to the whole group of five.

Using the same principle, you can set up a group alias for your class and enter the e-mail addresses of all the students in your class. (Remember, when you are using the e-mail address of somebody at the same domain, you have to enter only what comes before the @ sign, not what comes after. This can save a lot of typing!) What's more, all of your students can copy the group alias information into their own systems, and you will have a homemade class mailing list. This technique is also excellent for creating small e-mail discussion groups to complement the class list.

Class Newsgroups

A second way to organize out-of-class electronic discussion is by setting up a special USENET newsgroup for your class. To do so you would have to talk with the computer center staff at your college or university. One important question to ask is whether it is possible to make the newsgroup private, accessible only to the members of your class and not to other students in the university.

The advantages of a newsgroup over a mailing list (discussed in Chapter 2) are that all discussions are threaded (organized by topic) and that all postings can be held for the entire semester in the university's mainframe computer for the students to access at their own convenience. The disadvantage of newsgroups is that mail is not sent directly to the students' mailboxes. They therefore have to make the extra effort to go into the newsreading program and read the mail.

LEARNING ACTIVITIES

Whether you use a class mailing list or a class newsgroup, you can carry out the same learning activities.

Distribution of Class Materials

One very basic use of a class mailing list or newsgroup is as a mechanism for the teacher to distribute information, handouts, and materials. This method can save a considerable amount of time, paperwork, and photocopying. And because the students can print out the documents, store them electronically, and transfer them back and forth to each other, it can overcome problems arising from students misplacing documents or never getting them in the first place because of absence.

The real power of learning through e-mail and computer networking lies not merely in more convenient distribution of information but in helping build socially collaborative communication in the classroom. The activities below demonstrate how.

Collective Journals

Once you've set up a class mailing list or newsgroup, why limit yourselves to dialogue journals? You can incorporate whatever content you consider appropriate for a dialogue journal into a collective class journal. For example, if students are supposed to write one message a week regarding their attitudes toward English, their personal experiences, or their thoughts on a particular language-learning strategy, instead of sending that message just to you they could send it to the whole class via the class mailing list. Then all students would have the opportunity to interact and learn from each other.

At times students may want to share information privately with you. It's usually a good idea to allow and even encourage students to send you private notes, even if many of their journal entries are shared with the whole class.

Pre- and Postdiscussion

Another way of using class mailing lists or newsgroups is for pre- or postdiscussion on topics related to the class content. For example, if your ESL conversation class is going to be discussing ethnic relations in the U.S, before the class you could post some questions related to this topic to get students thinking. Or if your EFL reading class has read and begun to discuss a short story by John Steinbeck, why not continue the discussion electronically throughout the week?

English Circle

What do students do when they have questions about English grammar or spelling or punctuation? With a class mailing list, they can raise questions or problems about English usage with each other as soon as they come up. If the students can answer each other's questions, great; if not, you can always step in and assist.

Grammar Review

Kelm (in press) of the University of Texas at Austin suggests the following activity: Have students discuss topics all semester on their class e-mail list, changing topics every 2 weeks. Midway through the term, assign students in groups to look through the e-mail archives and find 10–15 examples of correct and incorrect usage of particular grammatical structures. The small groups take turns presenting minireview lessons on their particular grammar structure, using examples from the students' own writing to make their point.

Collaborative Writing

A class mailing list or newsgroup can greatly facilitate collaborative writing techniques, such as peer editing and joint composing. The teacher can easily post sample compositions for discussion and analysis. Students can then post their own writings for comments from their peers. This can be done between pairs of students, in small groups (using regular e-mail), or among the whole class (using the class mailing list or newsgroup).

E-mail is especially useful for facilitating joint composing, as it so easily allows students to send copies back and forth to each other so that two or more people can write or rewrite various sections of the same document.

IN-CLASS, REAL-TIME ELECTRONIC DISCUSSION

A third use of e-mail for a single classroom is in-class electronic discussion. This can only be done in a classroom or computer lab with a number of computers networked to each other. Note that it is certainly not a requirement to have a separate computer for each student. It's entirely possible and in some ways advantageous to have two or three students working at each computer.

There's an important difference between the electronic discussions that take place during class and outside-of-class discussion. In-class discussion should be real-time—synchronous—conferencing in which the messages sent are immediately posted to everyone else's screen. (Real-time electronic discussion is sometimes referred to as *electronic networking for interaction*—ENFI—a term coined and copyrighted by Gallaudet University. It also can be referred to as *computer-assisted class discussion*—CACD.) Therefore, you can't use regular e-mail (which often takes several minutes to arrive) for this purpose. You will have to use a special software program designed for real-time communication.

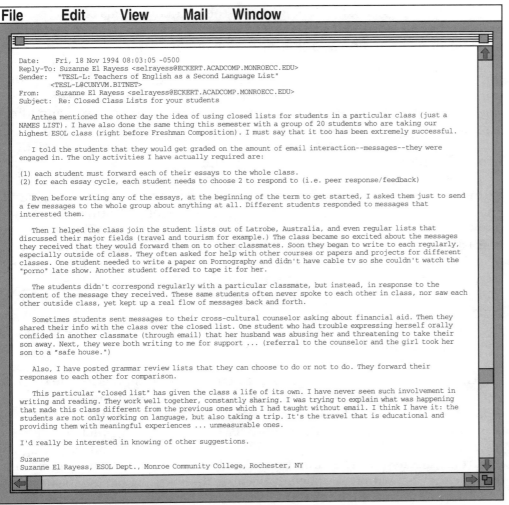

```
Date:     Fri, 18 Nov 1994 08:03:05 -0500
Reply-To: Suzanne El Rayess <selrayess@ECKERT.ACADCOMP.MONROECC.EDU>
Sender:   "TESL-L: Teachers of English as a Second Language List"
          <TESL-L@CUNYVM.BITNET>
From:     Suzanne El Rayess <selrayess@ECKERT.ACADCOMP.MONROECC.EDU>
Subject:  Re: Closed Class Lists for your students
```

    Anthea mentioned the other day the idea of using closed lists for students in a particular class (just a NAMES LIST). I have also done the same thing this semester with a group of 20 students who are taking our highest ESOL class (right before Freshman Composition). I must say that it too has been extremely successful.

    I told the students that they would get graded on the amount of email interaction--messages--they were engaged in. The only activities I have actually required are:

(1) each student must forward each of their essays to the whole class.
(2) for each essay cycle, each student needs to choose 2 to respond to (i.e. peer response/feedback)

    Even before writing any of the essays, at the beginning of the term to get started, I asked them just to send a few messages to the whole group about anything at all. Different students responded to messages that interested them.

    Then I helped the class join the student lists out of Latrobe, Australia, and even regular lists that discussed their major fields (travel and tourism for example.) The class became so excited about the messages they received that they would forward them on to other classmates. Soon they began to write to each regularly, especially outside of class. They often asked for help with other courses or papers and projects for different classes. One student needed to write a paper on Pornography and didn't have cable tv so she couldn't watch the "porno" late show. Another student offered to tape it for her.

    The students didn't correspond regularly with a particular classmate, but instead, in response to the content of the message they received. These same students often never spoke to each other in class, nor saw each other outside class, yet kept up a real flow of messages back and forth.

    Sometimes students sent messages to their cross-cultural counselor asking about financial aid. Then they shared their info with the class over the closed list. One student who had trouble expressing herself orally confided in another classmate (through email) that her husband was abusing her and threatening to take their son away. Next, they were both writing to me for support ... (referral to the counselor and the girl took her son to a "safe house.")

    Also, I have posted grammar review lists that they can choose to do or not to do. They forward their responses to each other for comparison.

    This particular "closed list" has given the class a life of its own. I have never seen such involvement in writing and reading. They work well together, constantly sharing. I was trying to explain what was happening that made this class different from the previous ones which I had taught without email. I think I have it: the students are not only working on language, but also taking a trip. It's the travel that is educational and providing them with meaningful experiences ... unmeasurable ones.

I'd really be interested in knowing of other suggestions.

Suzanne
Suzanne El Rayess, ESOL Dept., Monroe Community College, Rochester, NY

A TESL-L Posting About Class Mailing Lists

    Small groups can make use of a free, publicly available software program called *ytalk* (for computers networked via the UNIX system). Larger groups or a whole class can use Internet Relay Chat or schMOOze University, both described in Chapter 4. Or, depending on the particular goals of your program, it may be worthwhile to invest in a special software package to facilitate real-time discussion and sharing of documents.

Most real-time discussion software works on a similar principle. Usually the screen is divided into two parts. Everybody can sit at an individual computer and type messages on the bottom half of the screen. Whenever a message is sent, it immediately appears on the top half of the screen. Depending on the software, the comments will often be numbered and listed by name of sender. With commercial software, the comments can usually be sorted by name of sender or by topic if the reader desires.

More elaborate software packages may have a number of other special features that facilitate individual or peer editing and collaborative writing. For example, one software package, Daedalus Integrated Writing Environment, includes a real-time discussion component called InterChange, a set of heuristic guides for brainstorming, and another set of heuristic guides for peer editing (Daedalus software is widely used in composition, ESL, and foreign language teaching. For further information about it, contact Susan Meigs, *susan@daedalus.com*). These advanced features make these packages good buys, not only for teaching ESL but also for teaching writing to native speakers. Nevertheless, it is possible to get started on real-time discussion using publicly available software.

REAL-TIME INSTRUCTION FOR TEACHING WRITING

The most obvious use of real-time electronic discussion is for the teaching of writing. Students in general, and particularly second language students, often have a great fear of expressing their ideas in writing. To help overcome this fear and give their students as much writing practice as possible, some composition teachers conduct almost all of their course through electronic discussion. They find that the more students write, the more comfortable they get with it—especially because their writing occurs in such a powerful communicative context. Every word they put down is not for the purpose of being corrected by their teacher, but rather for the purpose of sharing ideas with their classmates.

Janice Cook teaches several ESL writing courses at Kapiolani Community College in Honolulu. All of Cook's classes are taught 100% on-line, with students writing back and forth together in pairs, in small groups, and as a class.

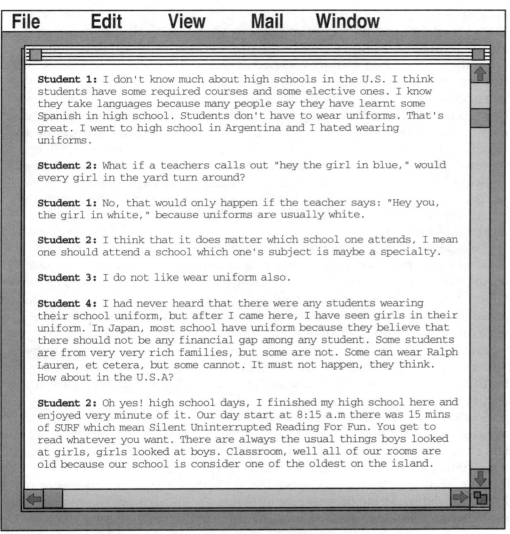

File   **Edit**   **View**   **Mail**   **Window**

Student 1: I don't know much about high schools in the U.S. I think students have some required courses and some elective ones. I know they take languages because many people say they have learnt some Spanish in high school. Students don't have to wear uniforms. That's great. I went to high school in Argentina and I hated wearing uniforms.

Student 2: What if a teachers calls out "hey the girl in blue," would every girl in the yard turn around?

Student 1: No, that would only happen if the teacher says: "Hey you, the girl in white," because uniforms are usually white.

Student 2: I think that it does matter which school one attends, I mean one should attend a school which one's subject is maybe a specialty.

Student 3: I do not like wear uniform also.

Student 4: I had never heard that there were any students wearing their school uniform, but after I came here, I have seen girls in their uniform. In Japan, most school have uniform because they believe that there should not be any financial gap among any student. Some students are from very very rich families, but some are not. Some can wear Ralph Lauren, et cetera, but some cannot. It must not happen, they think. How about in the U.S.A?

Student 2: Oh yes! high school days, I finished my high school here and enjoyed very minute of it. Our day start at 8:15 a.m there was 15 mins of SURF which mean Silent Uninterrupted Reading For Fun. You get to read whatever you want. There are always the usual things boys looked at girls, girls looked at boys. Classroom, well all of our rooms are old because our school is consider one of the oldest on the island.

A Real-Time Electronic Discussion Among ESL Students in Hawai'i

Students write about the writing process, discuss (electronically) things they've read, critique their own and others' work, and compose compositions together. Cook contributes to the process as a facilitator and guide rather than as an all-knowing expert. She has taught this way for 3 years and says she dreads even the thought of going back to nonnetworked writing instruction (personal communication, October 1994).

Pratt and Sullivan (1994) conducted a semester-long study on the effects of computer networking on teaching ESL writing at the University of Puerto Rico. They compared two ESL writing classes taught with the same syllabus but under different conditions. One class met one to two times a week in a computer-networked classroom where virtually all class discussion was carried out electronically using the Daedalus InterChange real-time communication software. The other class was conducted in a traditional classroom with oral discussion.

An analysis of the transcripts of large group discussions (one from each class) showed strong differences in participation patterns. Whereas only 50% of the students spoke up even once during the oral discussion, 100% of the students participated in the electronic discussion. Furthermore, in the oral discussion the teacher took 65% of the conversational turns, whereas in the electronic discussion the teacher took only 15% of the turns.

Pratt and Sullivan used holistically rated pre- and postwriting samples to compare the writing improvement of the two groups. They found that students in the computer-assisted class showed significantly greater gains in writing than did the students in the traditional class.

Studies of native speaker composition classes have shown similar advantages for computer-networked writing instruction, particularly for students who come into a course less skilled or confident about their writing. Hartman et al. (1991) and Mabrito (1991, 1992) have found that less able and more apprehensive writing students not only communicate more during electronic discussions than during face-to-face ones but also make more useful peer editing comments and incorporate more revisions in their own writing.

REAL-TIME GENERAL INSTRUCTION

The benefit of on-line instruction for *writing* courses is not surprising. But what about using real-time discussion in more general types of ESL and foreign language courses?

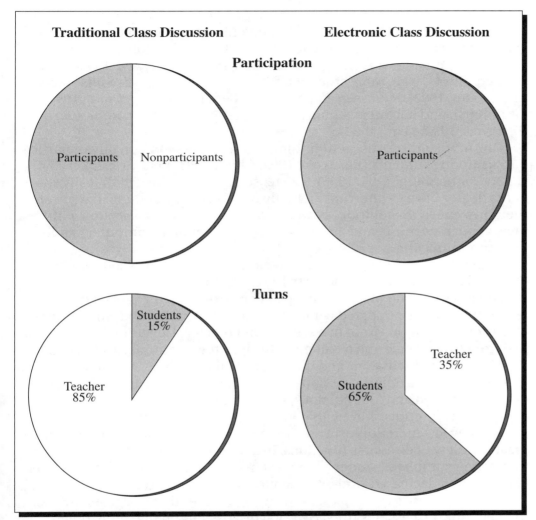

Traditional Class Discussion

Electronic Class Discussion

Participation

Participants | Nonparticipants

Participants

Turns

Students 15%

Teacher 85%

Teacher 35%

Students 65%

Participation Patterns in Traditional and Electronic Class Discussions (Pratt & Sullivan, 1994)

A number of studies have found substantial benefits from the use of synchronous conferencing in high school and university general foreign language courses, including faster-paced interaction (Kelm, 1992; Kern, 1993), a greater amount and wider range of language production (Kern, 1993; Kroonenberg, 1994/1995), more student attention to syntax and discourse features (Kelm, 1992), increased student-to-student interaction (Chun, 1994; Kern, 1993), and heightened motivation for target-language communication (Beauvois, 1992; Kelm, 1992).

One of the most consistent findings has been greater equality of participation among students (Beauvois, 1992; Chun, 1994; Kelm, 1992; Kern, 1993; Kroonenberg, 1994/1995). The reasons include the fact that shy students do not have to interrupt anybody or seize the floor but can write at their own speed. In addition, power and status markers associated with race, gender, position, and accent are less influential in computer-mediated communication

At the University of California, Berkeley, teachers of four-skill general French classes take their students to the computer lab for electronic discussion once a week and meet in the regular classroom on the other 4 days (Kern, 1993). Kern compared whole-class oral discussions and whole-class electronic discussions from two sections of French 2. He found that students had from two to three and a half more turns in the electronic discussions than in the oral discussions and that, more significantly, every student participated in the electronic discussion whereas in the oral discussion five students dominated and four did not speak at all. A sentence-by-sentence analysis of transcripts showed that in the electronic discussion students' language showed a more sophisticated range of morphosyntactic features and a greater variety of discourse functions. In addition, direct student-to-student interaction stimulated students' interest in one another, contributed to peer learning, and decreased students' reliance on the instructor.

Based on these experiences, Kern (1983) believes that it is generally best for electronic discussions to *precede* oral discussions on the same topic rather than the other way around. He finds that the first time students talk about an issue, they can get overwhelmed trying to simultaneously develop an idea, map it into an appropriate structure, pay attention to conversational turns, and deal with their own anxiety about their peers' and teacher's response. He believes that starting off electronically allows students to focus on the idea and take their time to express their thoughts without worrying about turns, pronunciation, or keeping the idea and its articulation rehearsed in memory. After the students have participated in electronic discussion, the idea has already been developed and articulated, and the students can focus on oral delivery.

At the University of Texas at Austin, Kelm (1992) brought his Portuguese classes to the computer lab once a week to hold electronic discussions of Brazilian short stories they had read. Kelm analyzed transcripts of an entire semester of electronic discussions in his fourth-semester Portuguese class. He found that students contributed 92% of the electronic comments (compared with 8% by the teacher) and that electronic discussions "are great equalizers" (p. 443) of participation. He reports that the students expressed themselves much more openly and honestly in electronic discussions than in face-to-face ones and reverted less frequently to their native language.

Kelm provides an interesting example of how he used the electronic transcripts to help locate and deal with students' grammatical errors. During the first seven electronic discussions, he found 32 examples of incorrect distinction between gerunds and progressive tense. After the seventh session, he excised all 32 examples for review. Following this review session, during the final 6 weeks there were only five incidents of this error, 82% fewer per session than before (Kelm, 1992, p. 451).

Chun (1994) of the University of California at Santa Barbara brought her 1st-year German class to the computer lab for electronic discussions 14 times over the course of two semesters for sessions averaging 20 minutes. She found that, in these 14 discussions, students directed 88% of their statements and questions to each other rather than to the teacher and that several of the shyer students were the most prolific in the computer discussions. Students performed a great variety of communicative functions in these statements and, over the course of the academic year, the ratio of complex to simple sentences increased from 1:3 to 3:4. In addition, "the types of sentences being written by students on the computer require not only comprehension of the preceding discourse but also coherent thought and use of coherent linguistic references and expressions" (Chun, 1994, p. 62).

Interestingly, Chun claims that although these *skills* are important components of written proficiency, the types of *sentences* strongly resemble what would be spoken in conversation. She thus expresses the hope that the writing competence gained from electronic discussion will gradually be transferred to the students' speaking competence.

Electronic communication is a valuable teaching tool in a single classroom. Using e-mail and electronic communication within your classroom can be excellent training for your students before you launch them into e-mail communication with other students around the world.

REFERENCES

Beauvois, M. H. (1992). Computer-assisted classroom discussion in the foreign language classroom: Conversation in slow motion. *Foreign Language Annals, 25,* 455–464.

Chun, D. (1994). Using computer networking to facilitate the acquisition of interactive competence. *System, 22,* 17–31.

Hartman, K., Neuwirth, C., Kiesler, S., Sproull, L., Cochran, C., Palmquist, M., & Zubrow, D. (1991). Patterns of social interaction and learning to write: Some effects of networked technologies. *Written Communication, 8,* 79–113.

Kelm, O. (1992). The use of synchronous computer networks in second language instruction: A preliminary report. *Foreign Language Annals, 25,* 441–454.

Kelm, O. (in press). E-mail discussion groups in foreign language education: Grammar follow-up. In M. Warschauer (Ed.), *Virtual connections: Online activities and projects for networking language learners.* Honolulu: University of Hawai'i Press.

Kern, R. (1993, November). *Restructuring classroom interaction with networked computers: Effects on quantity and characteristics of language production.* Paper presented at the meeting of American Council of Teachers of Foreign Languages, San Antonio, TX.

Kroonenberg, N. (1994/1995). Developing communicative and thinking skills via electronic mail. *TESOL Journal, 4*(2), 24–27.

Mabrito, M. (1991). Electronic mail as a vehicle for peer response: Conversations of high- and low-apprehensive writers. *Written Communication, 8,* 509–532.

Mabrito, M. (1992, December). Computer-mediated communication and high-apprehensive writers: Rethinking the collaborative process. *The Bulletin,* 26–30.

Pratt, E., & Sullivan, N. (1994, March). *Comparison of ESL writers in networked and regular classrooms.* Paper presented at the 28th Annual TESOL Convention, Baltimore, MD.

Tillyer, D. (1993). World peace and natural writing through email. *Collegiate Microcomputer, 11*(2), 67–69.

Wang, Y. M. (1993). *Email dialogue journaling in an ESL reading and writing classroom.* Unpublished doctoral dissertation, University of Oregon at Eugene.

4 E-Mail for Cross-Cultural Exchange

The most popular way of using e-mail for ESL teaching is for cross-cultural exchange. This chapter looks at many ways of bringing together students around the world, including pen pal exchanges, international student discussion lists, team-teaching projects, and international real-time simulations.

PEN PALS

Perhaps the most common way to use e-mail for international exchanges is through pen pal exchanges. Writing to pen pals electronically can have many of the same advantages that traditional pen pal writing can have: using English for an authentic purpose, making new friends, and learning about a new culture. Writing by e-mail has several additional advantages: It's fast, convenient, and either free or very inexpensive.

Pen pal exchanges can occur at any age or level. Leigh Zeitz of Iowa has her second and third grade pupils correspond with students in Australia, Mexico, and Japan. She reports that, after a Japanese exchange student was shot in the U.S., the children of several countries held a very involved international discussion about the event (personal communication, February 1994).

There are several ways to find partners for your students. One easy way is to send a message to TESL-L, TESLCA-L (computer-assisted language learning sub-branch), or TESLK-12 announcing that you are looking for one or more classes to do pen pal exchanges with your class. Another excellent place to look is Intercultural E-Mail Classroom Connections (see box).

Intercultural E-Mail Classroom Connections

Intercultural E-Mail Classroom Connections (IECC) is a great resource for finding classroom partners, looking over announcements of projects, or discussing general issues related to uses of intercultural e-mail. IECC is made up of four separate lists:

IECC: for teachers seeking partner classrooms. To subscribe, send the message *subscribe* to *IECC-request@stolaf.edu*

IECC-PROJECTS: for announcement of specific projects. To subscribe, send the message *subscribe* to *IECC-PROJECTS-REQUEST@stolaf.edu*

IECC-DISCUSSION: for general discussion about the intercultural e-mail classroom. To subscribe, send the message *subscribe* to *IECC-discussion-request@stolaf.edu*

IECC-HE: for making announcements and discussing projects at the higher education level. To subscribe, send the message *subscribe* to *IECC-he-request@stolaf.edu*

It's not necessary to look far away to have a successful pen pal program. Language learners in the same city have held many interesting exchanges. For example, Ethel Swartley of Philadelphia arranged for e-mail pen pal exchanges between foreign students and U.S. students on the same campus. She found this worked better than traditional conversation exchange partnerships, which often failed due to scheduling problems (posting on TESL-L, July 22, 1993). Tillyer (1993) paired ESL students with native speakers in New York and found that the students discussed a wide range of issues from prejudice to pedagogy to presidential elections. According to Tillyer, "The exchange gave the native speakers the opportunity to become experts on all sorts of issues and the ESL students had their chance to shine as international experts" (1993, p. 68).

Other same-city partnerships have included exchanges between immigrant ESL students and visiting foreign students and between ESL students and U.S. students studying second language acquisition. In the latter case, the exchange provided writing practice for the ESL students and case studies for the Americans.

Teachers who have used pen pal exchanges have reported two major problems: (a) lack of response and (b) lack of purpose.

Lack of Response. One major problem in pen pal exchange programs, whether on paper or by e-mail, is that many times a particular student's partner fails to respond. There's nothing more frustrating for students than seeing their classmates enjoy spirited international discussion while they stare at an empty screen! There are several ways to prevent this problem.

1. *Let your students get multiple partners from the same class.* Instead of pairing each student from your class with just one member of another class, why not pair each person with three to five partners?
2. *Do exchanges with several classes in different countries.* Give your students a real international experience by arranging a number of pen pals in a number of countries. If possible, let your students have some say on which classes they use.
3. *Set up a mailing list to group two (or more) whole classes together.* With a class mailing list, each person can write to everybody else. You can also set up a class list so that one person in your class can write to everybody in the other class, or everybody in both classes (or more) if you prefer.
4. *Have your students join an international e-mail discussion list.* Instead of pairing your students with individual partners, or even with another whole class, you might have them join international student discussion lists such as those listed in the next section. In that way, there are always lots of readers and writers from many parts of the world.

Lack of Purpose. A second major problem with pen pal exchanges is lack of purpose. Writing by computer to people in other parts of the world can be a very exciting experience, especially in the beginning, but for many students the initial excitement can wear off. Experience has proven that international e-mail exchanges can become lackluster if they are not somehow integrated into the curriculum of the course. For pen pal exchanges, this might mean giving your students some assignments connected to their pen pals, for example, to interview them on some specific topics and to write a report for the class based on the interview. More specific ideas about how to create a motivation for e-mail exchange projects are described later in this chapter.

INTERNATIONAL E-MAIL STUDENT DISCUSSION LISTS

Another type of program for cultural exchange involves international e-mail student discussion lists. These lists are similar to other international lists, such as TESL-L, but they have been set up especially for students.

The best known set of such lists is referred to simply as the *SLs*, or Student Lists. They are composed of the following nine lists for cultural exchange and writing practice among college and university students of ESL/EFL all over the world:

CHAT-SL	Student General Discussion List (lower level)
DISCUSS-SL	Student General Discussion List (higher level)
BUSINESS-SL	Student Discussion List About Business and Economics
ENGL-SL	Student Discussion List About Using and Learning English
EVENT-SL	Student Discussion List About Current Events
MOVIE-SL	Student Discussion List About the Cinema
MUSIC-SL	Student Discussion List About Music
SCITECH-SL	Student Discussion List About Science, Technology, and Computers
SPORT-SL	Student Discussion List About Sports

How the SLs Work

You can receive complete, up-to-date information about the SL project by sending a blank e-mail message to *announce-sl@latrobe.edu.au*. Here is a brief description of how the SLs work.

Teachers who are interested in participating are requested to contact one of the SL managers, Tom Robb, at the following address:

trobb@cc.kyoto-su.ac.jp

After providing some basic information (number of students, level of class, dates of term), teachers can register their class in the SLs. The teacher is then placed on a special list called TCHR-SL, where all partici-

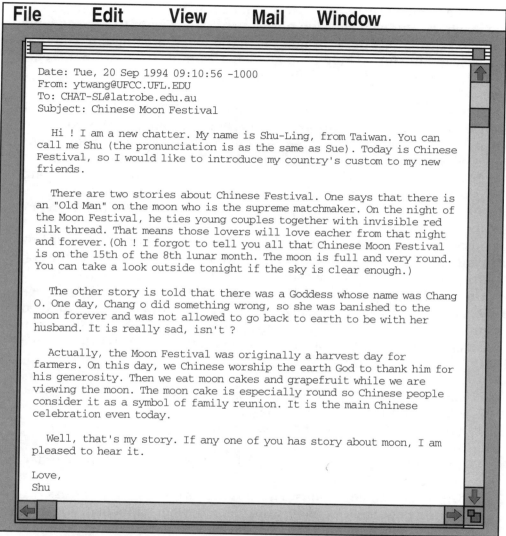

```
 File        Edit        View        Mail      Window
```

Date: Tue, 20 Sep 1994 09:10:56 -1000
From: ytwang@UFCC.UFL.EDU
To: CHAT-SL@latrobe.edu.au
Subject: Chinese Moon Festival

   Hi ! I am a new chatter. My name is Shu-Ling, from Taiwan. You can
call me Shu (the pronunciation is as the same as Sue). Today is Chinese
Festival, so I would like to introduce my country's custom to my new
friends.

   There are two stories about Chinese Festival. One says that there is
an "Old Man" on the moon who is the supreme matchmaker. On the night of
the Moon Festival, he ties young couples together with invisible red
silk thread. That means those lovers will love eacher from that night
and forever.(Oh ! I forgot to tell you all that Chinese Moon Festival
is on the 15th of the 8th lunar month. The moon is full and very round.
You can take a look outside tonight if the sky is clear enough.)

   The other story is told that there was a Goddess whose name was Chang
O. One day, Chang o did something wrong, so she was banished to the
moon forever and was not allowed to go back to earth to be with her
husband. It is really sad, isn't ?

   Actually, the Moon Festival was originally a harvest day for
farmers. On this day, we Chinese worship the earth God to thank him for
his generosity. Then we eat moon cakes and grapefruit while we are
viewing the moon. The moon cake is especially round so Chinese people
consider it as a symbol of family reunion. It is the main Chinese
celebration even today.

   Well, that's my story. If any one of you has story about moon, I am
pleased to hear it.

Love,
Shu

Communicating on CHAT-SL

pating teachers discuss various ways of making the SL project successful. The teachers' students can sign onto any lists they want to. One advantage of the SLs over many other projects is that the lists are ongoing and therefore easy to plug into. There is no need, for example, to coordinate schedules with specific teachers in other countries whose semesters run on different dates.

At the time of this writing, there are more than 1,000 students on the SLs from 35 countries, including Japan, Korea, France, Hungary, Mexico, Finland, Egypt, the U.S., and Canada. Lively discussions take place on a wide range of topics, with students quickly developing friends from numerous countries. Teachers or students sometimes launch special contests or events like puzzles, games, or "virtual picnics" to stimulate discussion. Students from a wide range of backgrounds and levels participate, from the barely literate in English to the near native. Many participants in the SLs find individual pen friends whom they write to separately (in addition to writing to the entire list), and these friendships have been known to continue long past the end of a particular semester or school year.

On the SLs, as on other e-mail projects, many teachers find that the project becomes most successful if it is integrated into the class work. For example, Ron Corio, a teacher in Virginia who has used the SLs in his classes, usually provides the following assignment (posting on TCHR-SL, June 7, 1994):

1. Join one of the SL lists.
2. Write a self-introduction to the list.
3. Write a certain number of posts to the list, for example, two per week.
4. Give information in messages to the list and ask questions in order to get responses.
5. Get at least three responses from students outside of your class.
6. Write a paper that explains what you did, what happened, and what you learned, and that evaluates the activity. Include three messages sent and three messages received in this paper.

Teachers participating in TCHR-SL discuss these and other types of ideas.

One special feature of the SL project is a student-published electronic newsmagazine called *Wings*. EFL/ESL students from all over the world contribute their articles to this magazine on a wide range of news, cultural, and social topics. The magazine is then distributed electronically via the SLs and elsewhere on the Internet.

To receive the latest information on *Wings* or on any other aspect of the SLs, send a blank message to the following address:

announce-sl@latrobe.edu.au

Another type of cross-cultural e-mail arrangement is the electronic team-teaching project. In team-teaching partnerships, classes in different places work together not only to share information but to complete certain tasks or projects.

TEAM-TEACHING PROJECTS

Sayers (1993), who runs a multicultural team-teaching network, describes three types of curricular projects that form part of many successful exchanges:

1. *shared student publications:* Students gather information in their respective locales and then share it. The articles are published in each area's local publications, or the students establish a joint editorial board and plan and publish a joint newsletter.
2. *comparative investigations:* The partner classes pick a theme of common interest, such as homelessness, drug abuse, or deforestation. Students then develop joint community surveys and other methods of collecting data. The classes write and share reports of their community's stand on the issue at hand.
3. *folklore compendia and oral histories:* Students gather proverbs, fables, folktales, and songs from their culture, often based on interviews with their peers or elders. The folklore of different cultures is then shared and compared (Sayers, 1993, p. 22).

Team-teaching projects can be organized in a wide variety of ways, ranging from simple projects involving two classes to very complex simulations involving numerous classes from many countries. There are basically two ways to get involved in a team-teaching project:

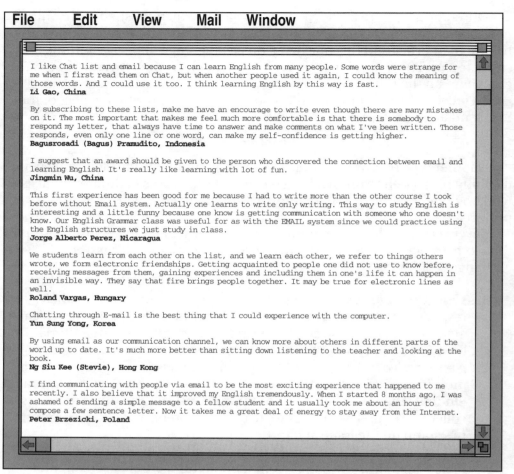

I like Chat list and email because I can learn English from many people. Some words were strange for me when I first read them on Chat, but when another people used it again, I could know the meaning of those words. And I could use it too. I think learning English by this way is fast.
Li Gao, China

By subscribing to these lists, make me have an encourage to write even though there are many mistakes on it. The most important that makes me feel much more comfortable is that there is somebody to respond my letter, that always have time to answer and make comments on what I've been written. Those responds, even only one line or one word, can make my self-confidence is getting higher.
Bagusrosadi (Bagus) Pramudito, Indonesia

I suggest that an award should be given to the person who discovered the connection between email and learning English. It's really like learning with lot of fun.
Jingmin Wu, China

This first experience has been good for me because I had to write more than the other course I took before without Email system. Actually one learns to write only writing. This way to study English is interesting and a little funny because one know is getting communication with someone who one doesn't know. Our English Grammar class was useful for as with the EMAIL system since we could practice using the English structures we just study in class.
Jorge Alberto Perez, Nicaragua

We students learn from each other on the list, and we learn each other, we refer to things others wrote, we form electronic friendships. Getting acquainted to people one did not use to know before, receiving messages from them, gaining experiences and including them in one's life it can happen in an invisible way. They say that fire brings people together. It may be true for electronic lines as well.
Roland Vargas, Hungary

Chatting through E-mail is the best thing that I could experience with the computer.
Yun Sung Yong, Korea

By using email as our communication channel, we can know more about others in different parts of the world up to date. It's much more better than sitting down listening to the teacher and looking at the book.
Ng Siu Kee (Stevie), Hong Kong

I find communicating with people via email to be the most exciting experience that happened to me recently. I also believe that it improved my English tremendously. When I started 8 months ago, I was ashamed of sending a simple message to a fellow student and it usually took me about an hour to compose a few sentence letter. Now it takes me a great deal of energy to stay away from the Internet.
Peter Brzezicki, Poland

Student Comments on the SL Project

1. Place your own announcement or appeal in a mailing list or USENET newsgroup to try to find partners.
2. Read the announcements from others on these lists and pick one that seems interesting to you.

Some of the best lists for reading or placing announcements include

TESL-L, TESLCA-L, TESLK-12, and IECC (see Appendix C for e-mail addresses). Some of the better-known ongoing team-teaching projects are the following.

The Email Project is an outstanding ongoing project, organized out of the Language Centre of Helsinki University of Technology, that brings together advanced English language students from a number of countries to work together on problems. In the 1994–1995 project, students from Finland, Hong Kong, Korea, France, Norway, and the U.S. formed multinational teams to work on one of three international activities: an environmental problem-solving contest, a cities project, or an international robot design competition. The international teams wrote up numerous documents as part of their research, including introductory letters, CVs, technical reports, abstracts, and essays.

For information on joining the Email Project, write to Ruth Vilmi at *project@hila.hut.fi.*

The Email Project

Project Icons is another multinational project, similar in some ways to a model United Nations. Students from countries all over the world form negotiating groups for specific countries (either their own country or another one they pick) on a specific topic, such as population control or global warming. The groups write and exchange position papers and conduct, via e-mail, multinational negotiations. These negotiations culminate in two 1-hour real-time international debates. A debriefing process follows.

Project Icons charges a fee for participation that may be waived under certain circumstances. For further information about Project Icons, write to *jw53@umail.umd.edu.*

Project Icons

The International Business Class mailing list (IBC-L) was set up by business classes from three U.S. universities in order to discuss a wide range of international business topics and to conduct some experimental special learning projects. The list welcomes partner classes in business from colleges and universities anywhere in the world. For information, write to *ddm2@lehigh.edu.*

IBC-L

A number of projects exist for elementary and secondary students as well. The International Education and Resource Network (I*EARN) brings

K–12 Projects

together more than 500 elementary and secondary schools in some 20 countries for a variety of joint projects including shared student publications, exchanges, and comparative investigations. For information, contact *iearn@igc.apc.org*.

The Global SchoolNet Foundation (*fred@acme.fred.org*) organizes numerous projects linking up workers all over the world, such as Newsday, Geogame, Santa Letters, Seasons, and Fieldtrips. In addition, the foundation offers consulting assistance to teachers who want to organize their own projects and helps publicize these projects through a number of LISTSERVs and newsgroups. The foundation also offers on-line training courses in Internet skills and sells handbooks and hardware helpful for computer networking.

A number of other organizations attempt to link school children around the world, including KIDSPHERE, K12NET, and EDNET, all of which are further described in Appendix C.

Finally, some of the large commercial on-line services sponsor their own education projects. In one of the best-known, America Online's Scrapbook U.S.A., U.S. students exchange essays, share postcards, and have real-time contact.

REAL-TIME CHATTING AND SIMULATIONS

Just as real-time electronic discussion can be a very valuable tool for in-class communication (see Chapter 3), you can arrange real-time discussion with partner classrooms in other parts of the world. Two ways to do so are through Internet Relay Chat (IRC) and schMOOze University.

Internet Relay Chat

IRC is a service that allows people from all over the world to chat together at the same time. It is made up of numerous channels, each with anywhere from two to dozens or even hundreds of people from all over the world chatting together. All those connected on a particular channel sit and type at their own computers, and whatever they send is immediately posted on the screens of all other participants. You can imagine that this creates quite a lively international conversation!

IRC channels are usually public, with different people in different places signing on and off at will. This activity creates a pretty hectic atmosphere—perhaps a little bit too hectic for people just learning English. However, private channels can be established on IRC. For example, your class and partner classes in other parts of the world could all join a channel at a specified time and then close it off to other people.

To use IRC, your system will need to have special IRC software. To find if you have it, ask one of your system managers, or get on-line, type *IRC* or *LIRC*, and see what happens. If you have a UNIX system, you can display the documentation for IRC by using the *man* (on-line manual) command. At the UNIX prompt, type *man IRC* or *man LIRC*.

If your system does not have IRC software, you can easily find and obtain it for free on the Internet. Information on how to obtain this and other software is found in Chapter 6. Further details on how to use IRC are found in some of the Internet reference books listed in Appendix A, such as *The Internet Complete Reference* (Harley & Stout, 1994).

One way that your class can connect live for real-time discussion with others around the world is by using schMOOze University, a special MOO established for ESL/EFL teachers and students.

schMOOze University

Basically, MOOs (see Chapter 2) are electronic facilities for real-time discussion and simulation. There are two basic differences between a MOO and IRC:

- Whereas IRC is like an open party line (although it can be made private), MOOs are defined by particular interest. If you join an open channel on an IRC, there will be all sorts of people from all fields and interests. On schMOOze University, there will only be other ESL/EFL teachers and students, thus creating a safer, more comfortable atmosphere.
- MOOs take place in a special simulated environment. In addition to chatting with people on schMOOze, you can move from one room to another, examine the objects in your room, create an identity, explore other people's identities, and play games.

To use schMOOze University, you will need to send a command called *telnet* to *arthur.rutgers.edu 8888*. (See Chapter 6 for an explanation of what telnet is and how to use it.) Once you are connected, type *connect guest*. The following are some commands you can then use within schMOOze:

Dorine Houston, who brings her students to schMOOze frequently, rec-

@who	gives a list of who the other people are at the MOO
@join xxx	puts you in the same room as another person
@go xxx	moves you to another place or room
look	shows you a description of your place or room
say xxx	communicates your message to all on the MOO (For example, if I typed *say Hello*, other people would see on their screen *Mark says "hello."*)
" xxx	same as *say* (no closing quotation mark needed)
: xxx	acts or emotes (For example, if I were to type *: smiles*, other people would see on their screens *Mark smiles*.)
@quit	exits the MOO
help	gives further information on MOO commands

ommends that, soon after you enter, you go to the classroom (by typing *@go classroom*) for 5–10 minutes in order to learn and practice some basic commands (posting on TESLCA-L, November 19, 1994).

Using MOOs can be extremely rewarding and interesting but also quite confusing the first time. You should definitely practice yourself a few times before bringing your students on. You may also want to consider bringing only a few students on at a time at first. Later, you can arrange special times for your students in your class to meet on the MOO with other classes or groups from faraway places.

Additional MOOs

SchMOOze University should provide most of what ESL/EFL students would need or want in a MOO. Here is a list of some additional MOOs and their addresses in case you or your students would like to go exploring:

FrenchMOO	*daedalus.com 7777*
MundoHispano (Spanish)	*io.syr.edu 8888*
COLLEGETOWN	*next.cs.bvc.edu 7777*
Global Village	*general.uoguelph.ca 8888*
Diversity University	*erau.db.erau.edu 8888*

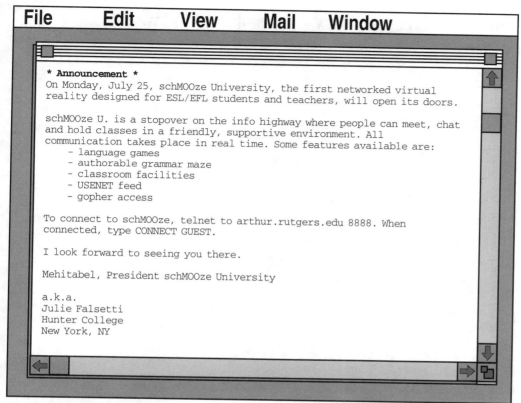

File   Edit   View   Mail   Window

```
* Announcement *
On Monday, July 25, schMOOze University, the first networked virtual
reality designed for ESL/EFL students and teachers, will open its doors.

schMOOze U. is a stopover on the info highway where people can meet, chat
and hold classes in a friendly, supportive environment. All
communication takes place in real time. Some features available are:
     - language games
     - authorable grammar maze
     - classroom facilities
     - USENET feed
     - gopher access

To connect to schMOOze, telnet to arthur.rutgers.edu 8888. When
connected, type CONNECT GUEST.

I look forward to seeing you there.

Mehitabel, President schMOOze University

a.k.a.
Julie Falsetti
Hunter College
New York, NY
```

Announcing schMOOze University

PostModernCultureMOO	*hero.village.virginia.edu 8888*
Virtual Online University	*coyote.csusm.edu 8888*
LambdaMOO	*lambda.parc.xerox.com 8888*
MediaMOO (teachers only)	*purple-crayon.media.mit.edu 8888*

You connect to these MOOs in the same way as for schMOOze. Once you are connected, type *connect guest*. Commands sometimes vary for MOOs, but the commands listed above for schMOOze are standard ones that should work for almost all MOOs.

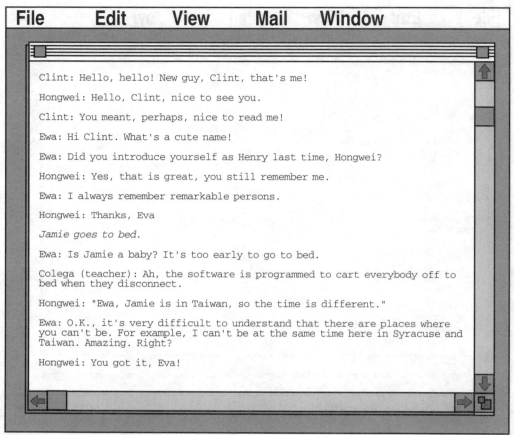

ESL Students Chatting on schMOOze University

MOO Clients

One feature that can make MOOs confusing is that what you type is mixed together with what you're reading. One way to avoid this problem is to use a special MOO client. A client will provide you with a special box on the bottom of your screen for typing your new commands, which makes using the MOO less confusing. Two of the most popular MOO clients are TinyFugue and MUDDweller. Ask your computer center staff if a MOO client is installed in your system. If not, you can locate and obtain updated versions using special Internet tools called Archie and Anonymous File Transfer Protocol (FTP) (see Chapter 6). Using a client is not a requirement for using MOOs, but it does make it a little easier for both you and your students.

Research studies on cross-cultural exchanges via e-mail are difficult to carry out, as they involve assessing the impact of decentralized, autonomous communication that takes place over the course of a semester or longer and that is often initiated outside the normal class place and time. Nevertheless, such studies are important if we are to understand the best ways to make use of this powerful new tool.

One of the most serious and interesting studies was conducted by Tella (1991, 1992a, 1992b) of the University of Helsinki, who carried out a 2-semester investigation of e-mail exchanges between four Finnish high school classes and their partner classes in England. Students in the two countries exchanged e-mails several times a month on a wide variety of personal and social issues from November 1989 to May 1990. Topics, chosen by the students, included holidays, hobbies, sports, pets, work, travel, music, television, poetry, literature, food, prices, war, refugees, and the environment.

Using an ethnographic approach that combined observations, interviews, and analysis of text messages, Tella carefully tracked all aspects of the cultural exchange, including where the team-teaching partners were located, how the project was launched, what kind of messages the students sent and received, how the relationships changed and developed over time, and how the students felt about the process. Comparing the results with the traditional Finnish classroom, he concluded as follows:

- The emphasis switched from teacher-centered, large-group-sponsored teaching toward a more individualized and learner-centered working environment. Students particularly benefited from being able to select their own themes and topics for interaction rather than having to follow the topics and themes of the syllabus, the teacher, or the rest of the group (Tella, 1992b, p. 244).
- The e-mail communication gave a good chance to practice language in open-ended linguistic situations. A shift from form to content was achieved, a free flow of ideas—and with it expres-

sions, idioms, and vocabulary (Tella, 1992b, pp. 244–245).

- The whole writing process changed to some extent. Rather than writing their compositions only once, as is the norm, the Finnish students naturally edited and revised their compositions, poems, and other messages to make them appropriate for their English peers. Instead of writing most of their compositions and other work alone, they increasingly made use of peer tutoring and other collaborative methods in order to compose their e-mails together (Tella, 1992b, pp. 244–245).

- The quality of writing improved as writing changed from teacher sponsored and led, only to be marked and graded, to real-purpose writing with genuine audiences around the world (Tella, 1992b, p. 245).

- The modes of writing became more versatile, including not only the narrative and descriptive genres usually found in the regular class, but also personal, expressive, and argumentative uses of language (Tella, 1992b, p. 245).

- Reading became more public and collaborative, with students actively assisting each other in studying incoming messages. Students also used different reading styles to read the wide variety of messages, notices, and documents that came in (Tella, 1992b, p. 246).

- The Finnish girls, who had fewer computers at home and thus were often disadvantaged in their use of them, participated equally and enthusiastically; their ease at writing and socializing with others helped overcome their traditional handicap with computers. On the other hand, the Finnish boys, who traditionally dislike writing, took to it very well; their enjoyment of computers and their comfort with informal registers of communication helped them overcome their traditional dislike of writing (Tella, 1992a).

Tella recommends that teachers pay close attention to what boys and girls master best in computers and try to develop activities that put to many-sided use the varying types of student expertise. He also urges that computing activities be incorporated into the school curriculum as early as possible to prevent any computer inequity developing as a result of differential access to computers at home.

Although Tella was referring specifically to differential access in Finland based on gender, it seems reasonable to conclude that in other countries his suggestion might be important for preventing inequities due to differential access based on factors such as race, nationality, language, ethnic group, or economic status. For an interesting discussion of this issue from a North American perspective, see Cummins and Sayers (1990).

Another interesting study was conducted by Barson, Frommer, and Schwartz (1993) of Stanford University, Harvard University, and the University of Pittsburgh, respectively. They analyzed several experiments between 1988 and 1993 in which two intermediate French classes from different universities joined together via e-mail to accomplish a semester-long task, in most cases the publication of a student newspaper or magazine. The long-distance collaboration was but one aspect of a general task-based orientation, with students also actively working collaboratively within small work groups in their own class. The specifics varied from semester to semester, but the general steps were the same:

1. Students were trained to use the computer system. All tutorials and handouts were in the target language.
2. Students sent out general e-mail messages discussing their interests until they could agree on and name a project (e.g., *Le Pont Français* [The French Bridge], the first collaborative Harvard-Stanford newspaper). Editors and assistants were appointed and began to take charge of the project.
3. Students on the two campuses divided up work and began researching and writing. Collaborative writing often involved students on each campus e-mailing drafts back and forth to each other.
4. With the teachers' assistance, students conducted peer critiques of articles from both campuses, and the articles were then edited and revised. With all work being done on computer, original drafts were often rewritten four or five times.
5. Final layout was done either separately—to give students at each site freer production reign—or collectively by sending the formatted document back and forth. Extra space was filled in by last-minute extra con-

tributions, such as surveys devised and carried out at one or both sites.
6. The publication was distributed and a party was held to acknowledge the successful group effort.

Although the study involved no native speakers of French, the researchers found very positive language learning and affective results. Interestingly, most of their comments are directed at how the project helped the students' speaking ability. Their conclusions (Barson, Frommer, & Schwartz, 1993):

- Students experienced the exchanges, negotiations, management talk, and discussions as authentic rather than pedagogic. The context required a spontaneous use of French that was far more typical of everyday language in a francophone country than anything taking place in a conventional classroom setting. As a result, students developed a facility for speaking in class freely and spontaneously, although not always flawlessly.

- The students experienced deep satisfaction at being able to "manage their life" (p. 582) in the target language with a fair measure of success. They came into a sense of their own responsibilities as leaders and contributors, learning how to carry on conversations that were often at very challenging linguistic levels.

- Students benefited substantially from the increased opportunity to practice their French outside the classroom. Some even continued to correspond by e-mail with their partners, in French, after the semester ended.

- Success was not uniform. Some students tended to rely heavily on others, leaving all the computer operations and communication to a partner.

- Traditional achievement tests may not adequately measure gains in communicative competence that can occur as a result of such an approach; it may be necessary to restructure test materials along communicative lines analogous to the projects being accomplished in order to reliably assess the state of the students' interlanguage. At the same time, individual grading is problematic for group projects in which there has been extensive collaboration and peer critique. In such cases, collective grading, though problematic, may be preferable so as to reinforce the importance of the project and the group effort.

In the above-described projects, the paired classes were truly team taught as a single unit, thus allowing the assigning of collective grades for projects even to team members from different schools. In some situations, it may not be practical to assign a collective grade to students from different classes or even different countries. One alternative is to make use of student portfolios in assigning grades (see Chapter 7 for an example). Another alternative is to ask the students to write individual papers reporting on their e-mail experiences or making use of information they have gathered via e-mail.

As a final note, many of the benefits described in the above two research studies could be achieved at least partially without the use of electronic communication. Language teachers successfully employed project-oriented, task-based, collaborative teaching approaches before e-mail was even invented, and they've organized successful team-teaching projects using mail, telephone, fax, and maybe even the pony express. Thus e-mail is not a magic wand that, once waved, replaces previous pedagogy. It is a powerful new tool that can help teachers *implement* good pedagogy—especially by facilitating collaborative cross-cultural exchanges such as the many creative examples described in this chapter.

REFERENCES

Barson, J., Frommer, J., & Schwartz, M. (1993). Foreign language learning using email in a task-oriented perspective: Interuniversity experiments in communication and collaboration. *Journal of Science Education and Technology, 4,* 565–584.

Cummins, J., & Sayers, D. (1990). Education 2001: Learning networks and educational reform. *Computers in the Schools, 7*(1–2), 1–29.

Harley, H., & Stout, R. (1994). *The Internet complete reference.* Berkeley, CA: Osborne McGraw-Hill.

Sayers, D. (1993). Distance team teaching and computer learning networks. *TESOL Journal, 3*(1), 19–23.

Tella, S. (1991). *Introducing international communications networks and electronic mail into foreign language classrooms* (Research Report No. 95). Helsinki: University of Helsinki, Department of Teacher Education.

Tella, S. (1992a). *Boys, girls and e-mail: A case study in Finnish senior secondary schools* (Research Report No. 110). Helsinki: University of Helsinki, Department of Teacher Education.

Tella, S. (1992b). *Talking shop via e-mail: A thematic and linguistic analysis of electronic mail communication* (Research Report No. 99). Helsinki: University of Helsinki, Department of Teacher Education.

Tillyer, D. (1993). World peace and natural writing through email. *Collegiate Microcomputer, 11*(2), 67–69.

5 Distance Education

Electronic communication can be used to teach those who, as a result of distance or other factors, do not attend regular classes. This chapter considers distance education for ESL/EFL students and for teacher training.

All the activities described in the previous chapters used electronic communication as a supplemental learning activity. Another purpose of e-mail is to deliver instruction to students who never (or seldom) attend class at all. This is often referred to as *distance education*.

There are many different reasons for establishing distance education programs. Perhaps the most common is that students are spread out over a great geographic distance and cannot attend class together easily. Other reasons might include lack of student or teacher mobility (due to disability or other reasons), lack of facilities for holding classes, or simply the desire to reach the greatest number of people at the most convenience and least cost.

Distance education is not a new phenomenon. Correspondence courses in a variety of subjects have long been taught all over the world. However, the use of distance education to teach foreign language has been somewhat restricted, as most people (correctly) believe that language learning involves the need for ongoing communication, and previous technologies made this difficult at a distance.

The use of e-mail and electronic discussion makes distance education for language instruction a much more viable alternative. However, the area is new and developing, with few established programs underway. Below are descriptions of a few programs that have been started for using e-mail in distance education of ESL/EFL students and for teacher training.

One very interesting model of distance education for ESL/EFL students was established by the English Programs for Internationals (EPI) at the University of South Carolina (Goodwin, Hamrick, & Stewart, 1993). Like many U.S. universities, the University of South Carolina attracts scholars and graduate students from international universities who come for degree programs or for research.

The transition process can be quite challenging for these international students. First, although they may have been using English for quite a long time, they are not necessarily up to the level in listening, speaking, reading, and writing required to succeed in a U.S. university. Second, they must make many cultural adjustments during their visit to the U.S.

To facilitate both language acquisition and cultural adjustment, the EPI established a prearrival distance education program via e-mail. Visiting students who were part of the Latin American Scholarship Program of American Universities (LASPAU) program were all invited to participate electronically in an orientation course for a period of several months before their arrival. The students completed a number of writing assignments, including, for example, their CVs and biographies, and were also sent (by e-mail) journal articles to summarize and analyze. In addition to the academic work, the students took advantage of the electronic connection to discuss with each other, and with the instructor, aspects of U.S. life such as weather, food, and accommodations. The program was evaluated as being very successful and is one of the factors that encouraged the EPI to expand their use of e-mail as an instructional tool in a number of their programs.

Another possible area for future development of electronic communication for distance education is in teaching composition. For example, George Wilkerson (personal communication, September 1994) and David Ross (personal communication, September 1994) both teach sections of college English composition in Texas via computer modem. Ross's students meet three times during the semester; Wilkerson's class never meets at all. In both cases

DISTANCE EDUCATION OF ESL/EFL STUDENTS

the classes are college English rather than ESL classes, but it is certainly reasonable to expect that ESL composition courses could be successfully taught in the same manner.

TEACHER TRAINING

In some ways, distance teacher training via electronic mail is more advanced than distance education for students. One example is in the state of Hawai'i, where the spread of the population to small communities over a number of islands can make centralized teacher training difficult.

To overcome this problem, the University of Hawai'i at Manoa established a special course for distance education training of second and foreign language teachers. The course is taught via interactive satellite television and e-mail. E-mail is used to transmit assignments, hold electronic discussions, post and discuss teaching journals, and collaborate on assignments.

This course also makes use of satellite television, but such advanced facilities are by no means necessary for successful distance teacher training. E-mail alone can provide a lower-tech way of accomplishing this task. For example, Alice Goodwin-Davey, one of the organizers of the above-mentioned distance education projects at the University of South Carolina, is now teaching at the University of South Africa at Pretoria, where one of her tasks is to train instructors in teaching academic writing. She is attempting to set up a distance education program using e-mail to reach out to and train teachers in various parts of the country.

Actually, electronic communication now makes it possible to get a master's degree in TESOL through distance education. One such program is offered by the Institute of Education at London University. For information, contact Anita Pincas (*teedapi@ioe.ac.uk*). The Institute also offers a special distance course in computer conferencing in education.

Graduate-level distance education courses are also offered by the International Society for Technology in Education (*iste@oregon.uoregon.edu*). A complete listing of their courses can be viewed via Gopher (see Chapter 6) at *iste-gopher.uoregon.edu.*

REFERENCE

Goodwin, A. A., Hamrick, J., & Stewart, T. (1993). Instructional delivery via electronic mail. *TESOL Journal, 3*(1), 24–27.

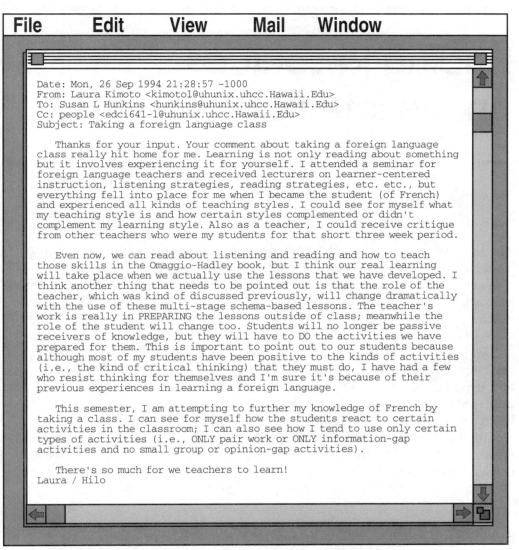

```
File        Edit        View        Mail        Window
```

Date: Mon, 26 Sep 1994 21:28:57 -1000
From: Laura Kimoto <kimotol@uhunix.uhcc.Hawaii.Edu>
To: Susan L Hunkins <hunkins@uhunix.uhcc.Hawaii.Edu>
Cc: people <edci641-l@uhunix.uhcc.Hawaii.Edu>
Subject: Taking a foreign language class

    Thanks for your input. Your comment about taking a foreign language
class really hit home for me. Learning is not only reading about something
but it involves experiencing it for yourself. I attended a seminar for
foreign language teachers and received lecturers on learner-centered
instruction, listening strategies, reading strategies, etc. etc., but
everything fell into place for me when I became the student (of French)
and experienced all kinds of teaching styles. I could see for myself what
my teaching style is and how certain styles complemented or didn't
complement my learning style. Also as a teacher, I could receive critique
from other teachers who were my students for that short three week period.

    Even now, we can read about listening and reading and how to teach
those skills in the Omaggio-Hadley book, but I think our real learning
will take place when we actually use the lessons that we have developed. I
think another thing that needs to be pointed out is that the role of the
teacher, which was kind of discussed previously, will change dramatically
with the use of these multi-stage schema-based lessons. The teacher's
work is really in PREPARING the lessons outside of class; meanwhile the
role of the student will change too. Students will no longer be passive
receivers of knowledge, but they will have to DO the activities we have
prepared for them. This is important to point out to our students because
although most of my students have been positive to the kinds of activities
(i.e., the kind of critical thinking) that they must do, I have had a few
who resist thinking for themselves and I'm sure it's because of their
previous experiences in learning a foreign language.

    This semester, I am attempting to further my knowledge of French by
taking a class. I can see for myself how the students react to certain
activities in the classroom; I can also see how I tend to use only certain
types of activities (i.e., ONLY pair work or ONLY information-gap
activities and no small group or opinion-gap activities).

    There's so much for we teachers to learn!
Laura / Hilo

Teachers in Hawai'i Distance Education Course Share Ideas via E-Mail

6 Finding Resources on the Internet

The Internet contains a wealth of information from archives, libraries, and data bases all over the world, including texts, graphics, sound files, software, and even full-motion video. This chapter will explain some tools for finding and accessing these materials and suggest information sources of interest to teachers and students.

An important use of telecommunications for language teaching is resource retrieval. The Internet includes the broadest array and the largest amount of information ever assembled on earth. And most of it can be accessed for free right from your home or office. To do so, however, you must learn a few basic Internet tools.

To make the most use of these tools, you will probably want to get a reference book on the Internet (see Appendix A for a list of several user-friendly books). In the meantime, the following is a brief overview of what these tools are and how you and your students can begin putting them to use.

FINDING INFORMATION AND MATERIALS: GOPHER

The easiest Internet tool for tracking down information and resources is called *Gopher* (as in having someone to *go for* or fetch things for you). The reason Gopher is so easy is that it is completely menu-driven: You don't have to memorize any commands; you just type *gopher* into your computer, press return, and wait for a menu to come up. After the menu comes up, you can move the cursor to select an item or category on the menu that you are interested in and continue the process.

Each Internet provider, whether an academic, commercial, or other institution, has a slightly different choice of items in its Gopher. Below is the opening menu of the Gopher on the University of Hawai'i's system.

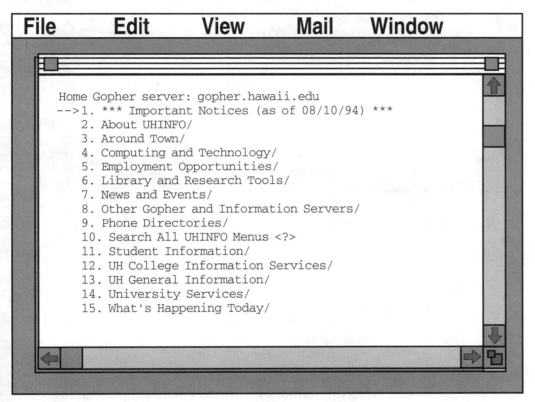

```
File        Edit        View        Mail        Window

Home Gopher server: gopher.hawaii.edu
-->1. *** Important Notices (as of 08/10/94) ***
    2. About UHINFO/
    3. Around Town/
    4. Computing and Technology/
    5. Employment Opportunities/
    6. Library and Research Tools/
    7. News and Events/
    8. Other Gopher and Information Servers/
    9. Phone Directories/
   10. Search All UHINFO Menus <?>
   11. Student Information/
   12. UH College Information Services/
   13. UH General Information/
   14. University Services/
   15. What's Happening Today/
```

Let's say you're interested in checking out employment opportunities. You would simply move the cursor down to Number 5, press enter, and see a new screen:

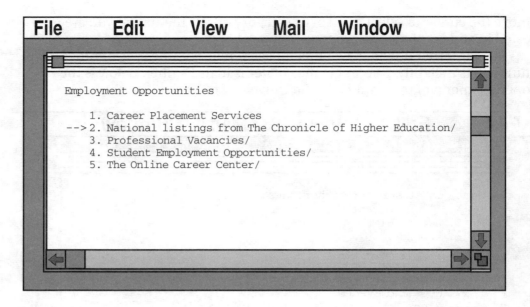

```
  File        Edit       View       Mail      Window

    Employment Opportunities

        1. Career Placement Services
    --> 2. National listings from The Chronicle of Higher Education/
        3. Professional Vacancies/
        4. Student Employment Opportunities/
        5. The Online Career Center/
```

If you continued the process by selecting Number 2, you could eventually get to several job listings in the field of ESL. The entire search path would be as follows:

> Employment Opportunities/
> > National listings from the Chronicle of Higher Education/
> > > SEARCH using the Chronicle's list of job titles/
> > > > Faculty & Research Positions/
> > > > > Humanities/
> > > > > > English as a second language/

Each slash (/) indicates a new level of the menu.

Gopher can save you a lot of time by allowing you to get poems, short stories, speeches, and other kinds of documents without leaving your home. For example, any of the president's speeches for 1994 can be found by following this path:

> Other Gopher and Information Services/
> > Interesting finds through the Internet/
> > > Information from the White House/

> 1994 White House Information/
> Speeches and Town Halls /

You can save yourself steps using Gopher by gophering to a particular site rather than starting at your own site. For example, if you want to reach the Alex collection of more than 1,000 on-line books, you can type at the system prompt

gopher gopher.ox.ac.uk

This will connect you directly to the Gopher at Oxford University. Then, to look at a lengthy list of on-line books, follow this path:

> The World/
>   Gopherspace/
>   Alex: A Catalogue of Electronic Texts on the Internet/

Then you will be able to decide whether you want to search further by author or by title. Once you find a book you like—or anything else in Gopher space for that matter—you can mail yourself a copy by typing *m*.

In addition to finding reading material for your students, On-Line Books can be a very useful source for building *corpora* (singular: *corpus*)—large collections of text that can be used to do computerized concordances or searches of how particular words are used in context.

One more convenient feature of Gopher is the ability to record a particular path you've taken so you can go there instantly in the future. Once you've found an interesting path in Gopher, simply type in *a* and press <return>. Be sure to type *a* while the arrow is pointing at the place you want to visit, not after you've already entered it; if you have already entered it, type *u* to go up one menu and then type *a*. Gopher will add what's called a *bookmark*. Thereafter, any time you want to see your bookmarks, type *v* for view. You can then instantly choose the complete path without having to go through all the intermediary steps.

Now that you know a little bit about using Gopher, you're ready to explore a real gold mine for English language teachers: the Teaching English as a Second/Foreign Language (TES/FL) archives at City University of New York (CUNY). Launched in 1994 by CUNY and the U.S. Information Agency, these archives contain a wealth of information, including journals, magazines, conference notes, abstracts, TESL-L archives, and announcements of employment and exchange programs. This is one Gopher site you will definitely want to add to your bookmark file!

The fastest way to reach this Gopher is by typing the message *gopher gopher.cunyvm.cuny.edu* at the system prompt and then selecting *Teaching English as a Second/Foreign Language*. If for some reason this doesn't work at your site, you can reach it by going through a long path of Gopher servers around the world until you get to CUNY. The exact path will vary slightly from system to system; here's one example of the path on the University of Hawai'i system:

Other Gopher & Information Servers
    Gopher & Information Servers via Univ. of Minnesota
        North America
           U.S.A.
              New York
                City University of New York
                  Subject Specific Resources
                    Teaching English as a Second/Foreign Language

Don't forget to type *a* while the arrow is pointing at *Teaching English as a Second/Foreign Language* to add that place as a bookmark for you to easily visit again by typing *v*. You will then see the following menu:

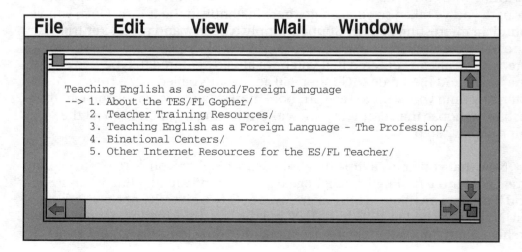

```
File        Edit       View       Mail      Window


   Teaching English as a Second/Foreign Language
--> 1. About the TES/FL Gopher/
    2. Teacher Training Resources/
    3. Teaching English as a Foreign Language - The Profession/
    4. Binational Centers/
    5. Other Internet Resources for the ES/FL Teacher/
```

You can continue to explore this menu by moving the cursor to any item you're interested in and pressing <return>. I recommend you set aside an hour or so to look around. From *English Teaching Forum* to *TESL-EJ* to CNN Newsroom Guides, these archives contain all sorts of information that you would look far and wide to track down otherwise.

Gopher is so easy to use that it can be a valuable resource for students as well as for teachers. David Tillyer of CUNY has his students retrieve movie reviews via Gopher in order to complete an assignment on adjectives. Here's a handout Tillyer has used with his students for this assignment, slightly edited to remove specific references to the CUNY computer system (personal communication, November 1994).

Using Gopher: Movie Reviews

Here are your instructions on how to get your own Movie Review to complete your adjectives assignment. This is your assignment:
1. Find a Movie Review in the Gopher at the University of Minnesota.
2. Save it to your file list.
3. Download it and print it.
4. Select at least 10 adjectives from it and circle them.
5. On a separate sheet of paper write the other forms of the word you can name (noun, verb, adverb). In a separate list, write the opposites of these adjectives.

Here are the instructions for finding the Gopher at the University of Minnesota:
1. Press {ENTER} to put your cursor on the command line (====>).
2. Type Gopher—check your spelling—press {ENTER}. (This is the opening menu for the Gopher. It is worth exploring. Look in subject-specific Gophers for material in your major.)
3. Use the arrow keys to go down to *Other Gophers*.
4. Select *Other Gophers* by pressing {ENTER}. (You will see another menu.)
5. Select *University of Minnesota Gopher*.
6. Select *Fun and Games*.

> 7. Select *Movies*.
> 8. You may TRY to select *Current Reviews*, but that selection is usually busy and will give the message *Not enough memory* or some other message. Try selecting 1993 and you will get a menu for months.
> 9. Select a month and then select a movie.
> 10. To e-mail yourself a copy of the movie review, type *m* and then fill in your e-mail address.
> 11. Type *q* to quit Gopher. You will be in your e-mail account again.
> 12. Download and print your review. If you wish, you can use the file on your floppy disk in your word processor to make the adjectives bold.
>
> If you have gotten this far, Congratulations!

SEARCHING THROUGH GOPHER SPACE: VERONICA

Although Gopher itself is extremely convenient and powerful, it is made even more effective with the use of a companion tool called *Veronica*. Veronica allows you to search through many Gopher menus around the world to find the exact reference you want. Most Gopher servers have Veronica built in so that it's easy to use.

Let's say you wanted to find a poem by William Blake but had no idea which Gopher site holds his poems. Using the University of Hawai'i Gopher server, here are the steps you would take to track down the information you need. First follow the Gopher path:

Other Gopher and Information Servers/
    Searching GopherSpace using veronica/
        Search GopherSpace (veronica) in SUNET (?)

At this point, you would be asked to type in a word, and you could type in *Blake*. This would yield you several dozen references to Blake that you could look through to find what you need.

CONNECTING TO OTHER COMPUTERS: TELNET

Telnet allows you to log in to a distant computer and access information there without dialing any long-distance numbers. All you have to do is log in to your own local system and, at the system prompt, type a two-word command. The first word is *telnet*. The second word is the node of the computer address you want to log in to. (The node is the part of the e-mail address that comes after the @ sign. For example, in my e-mail address, *markw@uhunix.uhcc.hawaii.edu*, the node is *uhunix.uhcc.hawaii.edu*.)

Telnet is great for checking your own e-mail when you are away from home. For example, let's say you are visiting a friend in another town. If she has access to e-mail, she can log in to her own local system (or give you the login information). At the system prompt, type *telnet yournode*. You'll then be asked to type in your password, after which you'll be connected to your own system. You can read your e-mail just as if you were at home.

Telnet can also be used for tracking down information. You can use telnet to get lots of interesting reading materials for your classes from the Electronic Newsstand.

To reach the Newsstand, at your system prompt type *telnet enews.com*. For your login name, type *enews*. No password is required. You will be automatically connected to the electronic newsstand, which is actually a Gopher menu-driven system. Here is the menu you will see:

Using Telnet: Getting Magazines On-Line

```
  File        Edit        View        Mail      Window

--> 1. Introduction to The Electronic Newsstand/
    2. Notice of Copyright and General Disclaimer -- Please Read.
    3. Magazines, Periodicals, and Journals (all titles)/
    4. Business Publications and Resources/
    5. Electronic Bookstore/
    6. Music! (8 magazines and 80,000 CD titles)/
    7. Travel, Trade Shows etc./ Lufthansa Takes Off/
    8. The Electronic Car Showroom(tm)/
    9. News Services/
   10. The Merchandise Mart/
   11. WIN A TRIP TO EUROPE SWEEPSTAKES/
   12. Search All Electronic Newsstand Articles by Keyword /
```

Now you can explore the Newsstand just as you would any Gopher site described above. Would you like to see a list of the titles of all the magazines, periodicals, and journals carried? Type *3* (or move your cursor there) and press return. Once you've selected a particular article you like, you can mail a copy to yourself (or to anyone else) by typing *m*. You will then be asked to type in an e-mail address, and the article will be sent there.

Using Telnet: Languages and Literacy Data Base

Another valuable on-line resource accessible via telnet is the information data base system of the National Languages and Literacy Institute of Australia (NLLIA). This system includes eight large data bases with information on courses, institutions, resources, language professionals, bibliographies, scholarships, and research reports related to languages and literacy.

Here are the instructions provided by NLLIA for accessing the data bases:

1. Type *telnet lingua.cltr.uq.oz.au.*
2. Log in as *dbguest.*
3. Type the password *NLLIA-db* (in upper- and lowercase letters, as shown).
4. You will get further instructions at this point. Generally you should now ensure that your terminal type is a VT100.
5. A small menu will appear. Select option 1 to access the data base system.
6. At the data base login screen, type in your e-mail address. This will give you access, as well as an automatic mail-back for reports you may generate.
7. The data base system copyright notice and then the main menu will appear. Select which data base you wish to access by typing in the appropriate number or by placing the cursor next to your option and pressing the space bar.
8. The search screen will appear. The bottom line is always the *HELP* line. This line changes each time you move the cursor to the next field. Whenever you see a *?* at the help line, it means that there is additional search help available. If you press *?* you will get another search window, with special tables you can access to help refine your search.
9. If you have problems, and want to get out of the screen you're in, use

the sequence *<esc> 3 <esc> 3* (press the <esc> key and then the 3 key twice). This will always take you back to the previous screen.
10.   To scroll up, use the sequence *<esc> 7*.
11.   To scroll down, use the sequence *<esc> 8*.
12.   *Always* leave the data base by going to the main menu and typing *X*.

TRANSFERRING FILES: FTP

Whereas Gopher is a tool for *finding* information, File Transfer Protocol (FTP) is special tool for *transferring* information. FTP allows you to copy files from thousands of different computers in all parts of the Internet. These files can contain not only text but also pictures, sound, and even full-motion video.

There is one catch to FTP. As in telnet, you must have access to the login and password in order to log on to the distant computer. This problem is solved with a special service called *Anonymous FTP*, which allows you to log on just by typing the word *anonymous* for the login (and, usually, your own e-mail address for the password). Once you log on, you can move to the directory you want using the *cd* command and send yourself the file using the *get* command. Here's an example.

Using FTP: Getting Song Lyrics

A great resource available by Anonymous FTP from the University of Wisconsin is the Lyrics Archive, a collection of thousands of song lyrics. Imagine, for example, you wanted to find the lyrics to "Ticket to Ride" by the Beatles:

1.   At your system prompt, type *ftp ftp.uwp.edu*
2.   When asked your login, type *anonymous*. When asked your password, type your full e-mail address.
3.   To change to the right directory, type *cd/pub/music/lyrics/b* (The *b* stands for the group you want, the Beatles. For another group, you would put another letter at the end.)
4.   Type *ls* to see a listing of all the groups and albums under *b*. You see the name *beatles*.
5.   Type *cd beatles* to get into the Beatles subdirectory.
6.   Type *ls* again to see what's in the subdirectory. You're in luck: You see *ticket_to_ride*.
7.   If you want to read the file to make sure it's what you want, type *get ticket_to_ride |more*

8. When you want to send the file, type *get ticket_to_ride*. It will be sent to your own home directory on your own system.

Commands for Anonymous FTP File Transfer	
Basic Commands	
quit	close connection to remote host, stop FTP program
help	display a list of all the FTP commands
help [command]	display a one-line summary of the specific command
get name-of-file \more	read a remote file
Directories	
cd [directory]	change to specified directory
cd ..	change to parent directory
dir	display a long directory listing
ls	display a short directory listing
pwd	display name of current directory
Transferring Files	
get [name-of-file]	download one file
mget [name-of-file...}	download multiple files
Setting Options	
ascii	(default) set file type to ASCII text (for basic text)
binary	set file type to binary file (for formatted files or most software, graphics, sound files, etc.)

Types of Files

FTP can be used to get not only text files but also other files such as graphics, photos, audio, video, and software. However, transferring nontext files is more complicated than transferring text because these materials are usually compressed or packaged together in some way to facilitate the transfer. The trick in determining what kind of file it is, how to transfer it, and what to do with it after you transfer it is to examine the file's extension (the last part of the filename, following the period).

Here are some basic guidelines:

1. If a file ends with the extension *.txt* or with no extension at all, it is likely a text file. It can be transferred and downloaded as an ASCII file, which means basic unformatted text. ASCII is the default setting for FTP, so you don't have to issue any special command.
2. If a file ends in *.sit*, *.cpt.*, or *.hqx*, it is a binary (formatted text, graphics, photo, audio, video, or software) file but in ASCII form. You can transfer it as a regular ASCII file. However, after you download it, you have to decompress it. Three shareware software programs are available for this: StuffIt Expander and Binhex (for the Macintosh) and PKZip (for IBM compatibles).
3. If a file ends in *.Z* or *.zip*, it is a binary file that can be decompressed directly within the UNIX system. First, transfer it as a binary file (by typing *binary* at the FTP prompt before transferring it). Then, after transferring it, type *uncompress filename.Z* or *unzip filename.zip* at the system prompt.
4. If a file ends in *.sea*, it is a *self-extracting archive*. Transfer it as a binary file (by typing binary at the FTP prompt before transferring it) and download it. The file will automatically decompress when you first open it.
5. If the filename ends in anything else, transfer it in binary mode and then decompress it. You will have to check with your computer center staff or and Internet reference book to determine the right decompression software to use. Alternatively, you can receive a comprehensive and up-to-date list of every decompression program and file type via Anonymous FTP. First FTP to *ftp.cso.uiuc.edu*. Then look in the directory */doc/pcnet*. The name of the file is *compression*. Fortunately, it is a normal text file, so you don't need to know any decompression information before you transfer or read the file.

Transferring Software

An excellent source of language-learning software is the Computer-Enhanced Language Instruction Archive (CELIA) located at both the University of Michigan (*archive.umich.edu, directory celia-ftp*) and Latrobe University in Australia (*ftp.latrobe.edu.au, directory pub/celia*). After logging in (*anonymous*) and moving to the correct directory (using the *cd* command), you can use the *ls* command to see which software is listed, type *binary* to set your system for a nontext transfer, then type *get name-of-file* to transfer it. Finally, consult the information above to figure out how to decompress it.

Searching FTP Space: Archie

What if you have no idea where to look for information you need? Just as Gopher has a search tool called *Veronica*, FTP has its own search tool called *Archie*. Archie will search through many Anonymous FTP sites around the world to look for the exact file you want.

Let's say, for example, you would like to get software to run Internet Relay Chat (IRC) as described in previous chapters. Assuming your computer system has an Archie client, at your system prompt you can type *archie irc*, and you will be sent a list of FTP sites that have IRC. You can then use Anonymous FTP to transfer the software. (If you have a Macintosh system, there is an excellent software program for running IRC called *homer*. Type *archie homer* and see what you find!)

If your system does not have its own Archie client, you can log on to any public Archie server. Choose the nearest one to you from the list below. For example, to log onto the Archie server at Rutgers University in New Jersey, at your system prompt type *archie.rutgers.edu*. For login, type *archie*. To perform a search, for example, to look for IRC, type *find irc*. If you need help in any way, type *help*. To quit Archie, type *q*.

A SMORGASBORD OF RESOURCES: WORLD WIDE WEB

Last, but certainly not least, is the World Wide Web (WWW). The Web contains several wonderful features that are rapidly making it more popular than all the other Internet resource tools combined.

First, the Web is a single integrated system that pools resources available from all the above options: Gophers, FTP sites, and others. It's a form of one-stop shopping.

Second, the Web has a full graphical interface. In other words, you can

Public Archie Servers		
Location	*Internet Address*	*Numeric Address*
Austria	*archie.edvz.uni.linz.ac.at*	140.78.3.8
Australia	*archie.au*	139.130.4.6
Canada	*archie.uqam.ca*	132.208.250.10
England	*archie.doc.ic.ac.uk*	146.169.11.3
Germany	*archie.th-darmstadt.de*	130.83.22.60
Japan	*archie.wide.ad.fp*	133.4.3.6
South Korea	*archie.sogang.ac.kr*	163.239.1.11
Taiwan	*archie.ncu.edu.tw*	140.115.19.24
U.S.: Maryland	*archie.sura.net*	128.167.254.179
U.S.: Nebraska	*archie.un1.edu*	129.93.1.14
U.S.: New Jersey	*archie.rutgers.edu*	128.6.18.15
U.S.: New York	*archie.ans.net*	147.225.1.10

not only read text, but also see photos, listen to sounds (including songs), and even view full-motion video directly on the screen.

Third, the Web is easy to use because it is based on a powerful concept called *hypertext*, which uses pointers to let you search for information within information within information. If you're reading a page and you want to find out more about something that is highlighted, you just point and click with your mouse, and you're connected to that item's page.

Why even bother to use the other tools, then, such as Gopher and FTP? In some cases, if you know exactly what you're looking for, FTP or Gopher might be faster. (Accessing audio or video information on the Web can be particularly slow.) And sometimes you can find things on FTP or Gopher that might not yet be connected to the Web. Finally, you need to have a direct Internet connection to use the Web (at least in its full graphical form), so many people might not yet be able to use it fully at home. Nevertheless, the Web is definitely the wave of the Internet future.

Using the Web

The Web is made up of tens of thousands of *home pages*. Universities, organizations, and even individuals can establish their own home pages that give an overview of the information provided. These home pages have their own special addresses called *Uniform Resource Locator* (URL). To use WWW, you connect to a particular home page you're interested in and then browse through it to see if there is any more detailed information you would like to access. Then you point and click on any highlighted word or sentence, and you will be sent to another page containing more specific information on that topic. You then look through that page for something else to point to, and so on.

To explore the Web, you need a special program called a *browser*. There are two types of browsers. The first is a multimedia browser, which allows you full access to all the types of data and information on the Web. You can use a multimedia browser only when you have a direct connection to the Internet. One browser, called *Netscape*, is currently available for free to academic and nonprofit users. Versions for both Windows and the Macintosh can be easily downloaded by Anonymous FTP from *ftp.mcom.com*.

The second type of browser is a *text-based browser*. It allows you to read all the text in the WWW but not to access photos, graphics, or audio. You can use a text-based browser even if your connection to the Internet is indirect. The most popular text-based browser is called *Lynx*.

To use the World Wide Web, you'll have to find out (a) whether your computer network provides access to the Web, (b) which browser it uses, and (c) how you can load and start the browser. The instructions in the box will show you how to use Netscape.

Using WWW: EdWeb

EdWeb is an on-line tutorial on education, technology, school reform, and the Information Highway. Designed for both teachers and telecommunication enthusiasts, EdWeb offers a vast collection of on-line educational resources, success stories of how technology is used in the classroom, a history of the development of the "Infobahn," and much more. The URL address for EdWeb is

http://edweb.cnidr.org:90

If you are using Netscape, you can reach EdWeb by clicking on the *Open* button and typing the EdWeb address into the box. (If you are using Lynx

Accessing World Wide Web With Netscape

The most popular browser for navigating the Web is called *Netscape*. The following are some basic commands for using Netscape to navigate the Web:

1. *Access information:* Position the cursor on any highlighted word or phrase and single-click the mouse on that point. This will take you to a linked document with further information on that word or phrase.
2. *Review previous pages:* To go back to pages you have looked at in this session, click on the *back* button at the top of the screen.
3. *Go to a new Web page:* Click on the *Open* button. Type or paste the URL address into the box.
4. *Go back to the home page:* Click on the *Home* button at the top of the screen to return to the home page from which you started this session.
5. *Create a bookmark:* A *bookmark* is a marker for a page you have visited in the Web that you might want to return to in the future. To save your current page as a bookmark, select *Bookmarks* and then *Add*.
6. *Go back to a page that you've bookmarked:* Select *Bookmarks* and you'll see a list of your marked pages. Select the one you want.
7. *Mail someone a page:* Select *File* and then *Mail Document*. Type in the e-mail address you want to send the page to (including your own, if you wish) and press <return>.
8. *Download a page (copy it onto your computer or disk):* From the *File* menu, select *Save as* and choose a directory where you want the file to be saved.
9. *View an alphabetical directory of subjects:* Click on *Net Directory*. Then scroll down and click on *Subject Catalogue*.

instead of Netscape, you can reach this or other URL addresses by typing *g*, typing the address, then pressing <return>.) You can then move through the

EdWeb pages. If you find something of interest, position the cursor on the highlighted word or phrase and press <return>. You'll be placed in a linked document with further information.

Using WWW: City Net

Rosen (in press) of the University of Wisconsin at Madison suggests the following activity for having students creatively use the Web—or, more specifically, the Web page for City Net (URL address *http://city.net*), which contains a wealth of tourist information, maps, photos, and even transportation information for cities and countries all over the world.

First, have the students browse through City Net and pick a site they'd like to travel to. Then let them consult with their families, friends, or even a travel agent to think of all the types of information they would need to gather to plan a trip. Next, let them come back onto City Net and explore in depth to find as much information as they can. Follow-up activities could be writing letters to consulates, making telephone calls to airlines, filling out passport forms, or creating a scrapbook including information printed from City Net and their own postcards, letters, and diaries.

For a more collaborative activity, divide the class into travel agents and clients. Let the travel agents use City Net to put together a travel package that would suit their clients' interests.

Let more advanced students follow up by using e-mail lists (see, for example, IECC and the Student Lists in Chapter 4 or USENET in Chapter 2) to try to contact people from that city and correspond with them by e-mail.

Using WWW: EXCHANGE

The Web can be used not only to provide interesting reading materials and informational resources for your students but also to give them a place and opportunity to publish their own work. One way to do so is through the student electronic magazine called *EXCHANGE*.

EXCHANGE is an "electronic, hypertextual, and cross-cultural ESOL magazine dedicated to publishing English writings of non-native speakers of English and providing quality learning resources to ESL/EFL learners throughout the World Wide Web" (Heidi Shetzer, posting on TESLCA-L, April 5, 1995). Its columns include World Cultures, World News and Events, Story, Learning Resources, Grammar Tutorial, and Conversational English. *EXCHANGE* seeks contributions from both ESL/EFL students and ESL/EFL professionals. Further information about how to subscribe and contribute to *EXCHANGE* can be accessed in the following ways:

- by WWW (graphical format): *http://www.ed.uiuc.edu/exchange/*
- by WWW (text only): *http://www.ed.uiuc.edu/exchange/exchange.html*
- by e-mail: contact Yong Zhao at *y-zhao@uiuc.edu*
- by joining the *EXCHANGE* mailing list. Contact Heidi Shetzer at *hshetzer@uxa.cso.uiuc.edu* (write *mailing list* on the subject line).

The possibilities for using the Web are almost endless. Here are the addresses of some home pages on the Web that you or your students might be interested in visiting:

WWW ADDRESSES

English pages:
http://english-server.hss.cmu.edu/
http://athena.english.vt.edu/favorite.html
language and linguistics pages:
http://www.willamette.edu/~tjones/languages/WWW_Virtual_Library_Language.html
foreign language teaching forum page:
http:/www.cortland.edu/www_root/flteach/flteach.html
applied linguistics pages:
http://www.bbk.ac.uk/Departments/AppliedLinguistics/VirtualLibrary.html
http://www.bbk.ac.uk/Departments/AppliedLinguistics/CILS.html
American University and ESL Information Service page:
http://iac.net/~conversa/S_homepage.html
education pages:
http://www.ed.gov/ed/index.html
http://sunsite.unc.edu/cisco/edu-arch.html
Intercultural E-Mail Classroom Connections page:
http://www.stolaf.edu/network/iecc/
K-12 Schools on the Web:
http://toons.cc.ndsu.nodak.edu/~sackmann/k12.html

> Canada's SchoolNet:
> *http://schoolnet.carleton.ca/English/*
> **current issue of** *Computer-Mediated Communication* **magazine:**
> *http://www.rpi.edu/~decemj/cmc/mag/current/toc.html*
> **back issues of** *Computer-Mediated Communication* **magazine:**
> *http://www.rpi.edu/~decemj/cmc/mag/archive.html*
> **an interesting report on the Email Project:**
> *http://www.hut.fi/~rvilmi/email-project.html*
> **Purdue University Online Writing Lab (with nice handouts):**
> *http://owl.trc.purdue.edu/*
> **Midlink Magazine: The Electronic Magazine by and for Kids:**
> *http://longwood.cs.ucf.edu/~MidLink*
> **ESL pages:**
> *http://www.educ.wsu.edu/esl/esl.html*
> *http://www.ed.uiuc.edu/edpsy-387/rongchang-li/esl/*
> **fun and recreation:**
> *http://w3.eeb.ele.tue.nl/mpeg/index.html* (MPEG Movie Archives)
> *http://alpha.acast.nova.edu/movies.html* (movies and television)
> *http://sunsite.unc.edu/Dave/drfun.html* (Dr. Fun page)
> *http://mistral.enst.fr/~pioch/louvre/* (the Louvre Museum)
> *http://sunsite/unc.edu/ianc/index.html* (Internet Underground Music Archive)
> **schMOOze University:** *http://arthur.rutgers.edu.8888*
> **Student List project:** *http://www.latrobe.edu.au/gse/sl/index.html*

A special e-mail discussion list will give you further information on the use of the World Wide Web in education. To join, send the message *subscribe wwwedu yourfirstname yourlastname* to *listserv@k12.cnidr.org*.

THE PURDUE ONLINE WRITING LAB

Increasingly, on-line resources are available using several different methods. One example is the Purdue Online Writing Lab (OWL), which makes its handouts and materials available through Gopher, World Wide Web, and FTP, and which provides free consulting for writing problems via e-mail. The box contains a self-description of services offered by this helpful project.

Another very helpful on-line writing service, staffed with 10 "cybertutors," is the University of Missouri's Online Writery. Contact *writing@showme.missouri.edu* for more information.

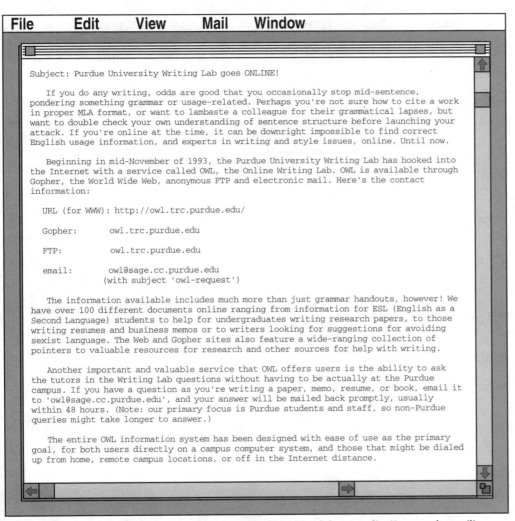

File   Edit   View   Mail   Window

Subject: Purdue University Writing Lab goes ONLINE!

If you do any writing, odds are good that you occasionally stop mid-sentence, pondering something grammar or usage-related. Perhaps you're not sure how to cite a work in proper MLA format, or want to lambaste a colleague for their grammatical lapses, but want to double check your own understanding of sentence structure before launching your attack. If you're online at the time, it can be downright impossible to find correct English usage information, and experts in writing and style issues, online. Until now.

Beginning in mid-November of 1993, the Purdue University Writing Lab has hooked into the Internet with a service called OWL, the Online Writing Lab. OWL is available through Gopher, the World Wide Web, anonymous FTP and electronic mail. Here's the contact information:

URL (for WWW): http://owl.trc.purdue.edu/

Gopher: owl.trc.purdue.edu

FTP: owl.trc.purdue.edu

email: owl@sage.cc.purdue.edu
               (with subject 'owl-request')

The information available includes much more than just grammar handouts, however! We have over 100 different documents online ranging from information for ESL (English as a Second Language) students to help for undergraduates writing research papers, to those writing resumes and business memos or to writers looking for suggestions for avoiding sexist language. The Web and Gopher sites also feature a wide-ranging collection of pointers to valuable resources for research and other sources for help with writing.

Another important and valuable service that OWL offers users is the ability to ask the tutors in the Writing Lab questions without having to be actually at the Purdue campus. If you have a question as you're writing a paper, memo, resume, or book, email it to 'owl@sage.cc.purdue.edu', and your answer will be mailed back promptly, usually within 48 hours. (Note: our primary focus is Purdue students and staff, so non-Purdue queries might take longer to answer.)

The entire OWL information system has been designed with ease of use as the primary goal, for both users directly on a campus computer system, and those that might be dialed up from home, remote campus locations, or off in the Internet distance.

Source: Taylor, D. (1994, November 28). *Purdue University Writing lab goes online!* [personal e-mail]. Purdue University, Department of Education.

Compared with other modes of communication, such as radio, television, and the telephone, the Internet is in its infancy. Thus many of its features are still somewhat complicated to use. Most of what you will want to do for language teaching may not require any of the special tools described in this chapter. However, if you want to quickly access a wide range of language-teaching materials from your own computer and help your students learn the research and resource retrieval techniques that will benefit both their studies and their career, you may well consider it worthwhile to learn to use some of these tools.

REFERENCE

Rosen, L. (in press). City Net: Travel the world from your desktop. In M. Warschauer (Ed.), *Virtual connections: Online activities and projects for networking language learners.* Honolulu: University of Hawai'i, Second Language Teaching and Curriculum Center.

7 Putting It All Together

This chapter discusses some principles for implementing the ideas from this book and some concrete models of instruction that integrate electronic communication into English teaching.

E-mail and other forms of electronic communication are a valuable tool for English teaching. Yet e-mail, like other forms of technology, will not itself solve problems. It will be up to you, the teacher, to develop the right ways of using e-mail based on your general goals, your teaching style and approach, an analysis of your students' needs, and the technological tools you have at hand.

The array of tips and suggestions here comes from others who have used e-mail in their classrooms. The guidelines cover four interfaces: student-machine, teacher-teacher, teacher-student, and student-student.

Even for English teachers—who are commonly excellent speakers of English, skilled typists, and experienced users of word-processing and other computer applications—using e-mail can be a confusing experience at first. Therefore, don't underestimate the confusion that students can experience when first attempting to use this new tool. The point is not to avoid using e-mail but to set up the experience so that it is empowering for students rather than frustrating.

IMPLEMENTATION: GENERAL PRINCIPLES

Student-Machine

The goal should be to make students autonomous users. The more they can learn how to do themselves, without having to always depend on the teacher, the more pleasure and satisfaction they'll get out of the process. Some general tips follow. (For more tips, see Robb & Tillyer, 1994.)

Before class meets:

1. Try to work with the school to make sure that any computers are as accessible as possible. The more frequent access your students have to the computers, the more rewards they will get out of using e-mail.
2. If you have any choice of either hardware or software, choose the ones that are most user-friendly. In educational settings, an easy-to-use system is usually preferable to a powerful but complicated one.
3. Prepare a thorough and easy-to-read handout for your students that covers all the basic instructions (see Robb & Tillyer, 1994).
4. Try to arrange for a couple of assistants the first time you introduce e-mail. It's hard to get around to many different terminals at the same time (see Robb & Tillyer, 1994).
5. Send a message to your students before they log on the first time. That way, they'll have something there waiting for them, which can really motivate them (see Robb & Tillyer, 1994).
6. Do a sample training session with one or two students first, so you can see what problems arise before you try to train a whole class (see Robb & Tillyer, 1994).

While training, teach your students how to (Robb & Tillyer, 1994):

1. send messages to each other as a first step
2. send you a copy, at least at first
3. send themselves a copy
4. forward messages to you or to others
5. print out messages
6. download messages they receive
7. prepare, save, and upload messages from a word-processing program

On an ongoing basis:

1. Include regular discussions about how the students are using the system, what problems they are having, what suggestions they might have, and so forth.
2. Train the students how to use the more advanced features of the system.

The following are some important steps to take if you are engaging in a team-teaching project with one or more teachers.

Teacher–Teacher

1. Choose a team-teaching partner who you know is reliable and dependable. Even if the person is a new contact that you meet through a mailing list, make sure the person answers mail regularly and seems committed to the project (see Sayers, 1993).
2. Discuss the goals that both of you have. It's not necessarily important that you have the same goals, but you should know what each other's goals are (see Sayers, 1993).
3. If more than two teachers are working together on a project, set up a special mailing list so that the teachers can collectively discuss any ideas about how to best carry out the project.

Many educators (Barson, Frommer, & Schwartz, 1993; Batson, 1988; DiMatteo, 1990, 1991; Faigley, 1990; Paramskas, 1993; Susser, 1993; Warschauer, Turbee, & Roberts, 1994) have noted that electronic communication can help foster a new teacher-student relationship, with the students becoming more autonomous and the teacher becoming more of a facilitator. Here are some suggestions for making this new relationship successful:

Teacher-Student

1. Decide ahead of time whether you will be reading your students' messages and let them know one way or the other. It is best not to be surreptitious (see Robb & Tillyer, 1994).
2. Encourage student autonomy and independence, but stay very actively involved yourself. The students are depending on your advice, experience, and direction in many areas (Janangelo, 1991; Warschauer et al., 1994).

3. Be a guide for your students not only on how to use the machines but on how to communicative effectively using e-mail. Discuss together some examples of effective and ineffective messages and what makes them so.
4. As in any activity, pay attention to those who are quieter and participating less. Sometimes it's fine to lurk (read messages without posting), but if you would like quieter students to participate more, try to find out what's holding them back and encourage them.
5. Be clear with the students about how their e-mail work will factor into their grades or evaluation. It's generally recommended that all students be required to send and receive e-mail as part of their assignment.

Student-Student

In the end, the purpose of e-mail in education is to foster more effective student-student communication. Here are some suggestions to help make that happen.

1. Help your students create a hospitable space and a sense of community. In the beginning of any e-mail relationship, encourage the students to introduce themselves, discuss aspects of their personal interests, and use the friendly, informal language and greetings that are common in e-mail (Bruce Roberts, personal communication, August 1994).
2. If you're doing a team-teaching project, arrange for other types of communication besides e-mail. For example, before the electronic communication begins, consider exchanging cultural packages made up of student photos, artwork, school newspapers, and other memorabilia (Sayers, 1993).
3. As much as possible, try to include collaborative, task-based learning projects. Beyond having the students just talk to each other, get them working together on exciting, meaningful projects that will give them a sense of involvement and accomplishment (Barson et al., 1993).

Nearly all teachers who have used e-mail in the classroom stress that results are best when the e-mail activities are well integrated into the classroom process. Bruce Roberts, one of the coordinators of the Intercultural E-Mail Classroom Connections program, explained, "There is a significant difference in educational outcome depending on whether a teacher chooses to incorporate email classroom connections as 1) an ADD-ON process, like one would include a guest speaker, or 2) an INTEGRATED process, in the way one would include a new textbook. The email classroom connection seems sufficiently complex and time consuming that if there are goals beyond merely having each student send a letter to a person at a distant school, the ADD-ON approach can lead to frustration and less-than-expected academic results—the necessary time and resources come from other things that also need to be done. On the other hand, when the email classroom connection processes are truly integrated into the ongoing structure of homework and student classroom interaction, then the results can be educationally transforming" (Bruce Roberts, posting on IECC-discussion@stolaf.edu, March 22, 1994).

How do you successfully integrate electronic communication into your class? Following are a few examples of how some teachers have done so.

In a high school class in Hong Kong, Kroonenberg (1994/1995) incorporates in-class and out-of-class electronic discussion in a way that she feels greatly facilitates the learning process. The high school has a networked computer lab where students can drop in after school or at lunch. The computer operators and teachers have established a bulletin board system at the lab so that students can post electronic messages to a class bulletin board.

Early in the semester, Kroonenberg assigns topics for out-of-class electronic discussion. She tries to pick themes that will be of direct and personal interest to the students, such as a controversy that had erupted in the school regarding student alcohol consumption. Students are to write at least one entry a week in what becomes a public journal. In Kroonenberg's responses to the journals, she attempts to use terminology that can enlarge the students' vocabulary. She also models grammatical structures that students have trouble with or that they have recently been working on.

Kroonenberg also uses the system to let students decide the topics for oral class discussion. Each student is required to (electronically) propose a

SOME MODELS

A Course Involving One-Class Electronic Discussion

discussion topic and read the proposals of eight other students. She feels that this helps guarantee that everyone's opinion is heard loud and clear. To reinforce this process, she also sometimes prints out and distributes copies of all the students' opinions.

On-Line Chatting. Occasionally Kroonenberg takes the whole class to the computer lab for real-time electronic discussion. Students are assigned partners and given opposing sides of an issue to argue and defend. Using special real-time software, the students write back and forth to each other, debating their topic. She finds that this rapid exchange improves not only the students' writing but also their speaking, as they are forced to read and comprehend quickly in order to participate in the discussion.

From Computer to Classroom. All the work on computer is closely tied to oral discussions. The topics selected or debated on computer are later re-introduced for classroom oral discussion. These discussions are usually quite lively, and the fact that the students are building on all the thinking and writing that has already taken place enhances the quality of the discussion. Kroonenberg says that the students' interest in listening is also enhanced; they often listen as intently as they viewed computer screens during chat mode.

Furthermore, Kroonenberg finds that students who are usually timid participate more actively not only in the electronic discussions, but in the ensuing oral discussions as well. Once they have had a chance to get their thoughts on paper for collective consideration, they are more engaged in the process and can contribute more easily and naturally.

Assessment. Students are required to complete all e-mail work, but it is neither corrected nor graded. Rather, it becomes part of students' portfolios and self-assessment process. Based on their portfolios and oral/aural work, students write a self-assessment in which they comment on their language skills and suggest strategies for improving these skills during the following marking period. In an ensuing conference, the student and teacher look over the collection of e-mail writing to see how the student's writing, thinking, and debate skills have developed during the quarter. Kroonenberg then comes up with a mutually agreed-upon action plan for each student for the following quarter. She also analyzes her own set of e-mail printouts in order to track class progress as a whole and decide where she needs to reinforce grammatical structures and vocabulary.

Teachers in Singapore and Canada organized an exchange project in English between a high school of Chinese-speaking students in Singapore and a high school of French-speaking students in Quebec (Soh & Soon, 1991). Students in each school used e-mail to exchange messages first with individual partners from the other school and later with small groups of students from both schools.

In the early stages of the projects, students engaged in electronic small talk, asking and answering questions about topics such as movies, television, teenage fashion, sports, and hobbies. Soon, though, the discussions moved to more serious issues, such as pollution and the ozone level.

Literary Texts. After a trial period of 3 months, the Quebec and Singapore teachers decided to attempt to more fully integrate the language curriculum. As a result, two literature texts—one from each country—were chosen for interactive learning. The texts included both traditional folktales and contemporary fiction. The goal was to use the reading and discussion of these texts to help students learn about distant countries with cultures and traditions far removed from their own.

In Quebec and Singapore, the students first read selections from both sets of stories with their teachers. They then electronically discussed the stories with small groups of students from the two schools, sharing their first impressions and questions. Students at each site also prepared and e-mailed or faxed background material that they thought would help the other students better understand the stories. Finally, they devised and completed assignments for each other based on the texts.

Students responded to the stories in a number of creative ways. They wrote essays, created small plays, developed debating points, devised background notes, and wrote poems.

Benefits. The teachers felt that there were numerous benefits to the exchange. They observed that the students

- learned to look at and assess their work and others' work from a new perspective
- learned to write more clear and effective prose in order to convey their ideas
- gained insight into the culture of another country

- gained a better understanding of the use of the computer as a communicative tool

These benefits would be impressive enough for any high school composition class. What is even more impressive is that all the work was carried out in English, the foreign language being studied in each of the two classes.

A Course Based on an International Multiteam Project

Ruth Vilmi teaches general English, business English, and technical English at Helsinki University of Technology (personal communication, October 1994). She has started a number of international team-teaching projects in order to create authentic writing situations for her students.

In fall 1994, Vilmi's students worked on two international projects: a robot-design competition and an environmental design competition. Vilmi found partner teachers for these projects by posting notices on various international mailing lists such as TESLCA-L (the computer-assisted language learning branch of TESL-L).

For the robot activity, Vilmi's technical English class was joined by university classes from Paris (taught by Linda Thalman) and Hong Kong (taught by George C. K. Jor). The classes were divided into teams made up of students from all three universities.

The project kicked off with all the students writing individual introductory letters and CVs for their teammates. Then the students worked together to design an award-winning robot for an international competition. Over the course of the semester they had to collectively complete five writing assignments, including

- a definition of the problem and why it needed to be solved
- a promotional brochure, including a narrative description of their robot, specifications, instructions, technical drawings, and price
- a letter to an appropriate company or organization regarding its plans to sell the robot
- a 250-word abstract of a call for papers for "The Fifth International Conference on Robots and Applications" to be held in Long Beach, California, March 8–10, 1995

- a record of how the group work was distributed (who did what, when, and how)

Finally, the students completed one more individual assignment: a 250-word essay evaluating the project. In Vilmi's class, students also gave oral reports at a "robot fair," where the team was the consulting group recommending the robot in question and the class was the company that had to decide which robot to buy.

The project was organized as a true competition, with the students themselves (from all three universities) determining both the voting procedure and the balance of the student-teacher vote. In the end, the winning entry was posted on World Wide Web so that teachers, students—and engineers—all over the world could have a look.

The expected learning outcomes for a project of this magnitude are almost too numerous to mention, but note at least that the students get authentic, highly motivating, and realistic practice in the exact kind of technical writing (abstracts, reports, brochures) they will need in their careers. The scope of the project even requires the students to develop very specialized (and highly useful) skills, such as scanning technical drawings into a computer and then transferring them by e-mail.

Vilmi's motto, which she includes in her e-mail signature, is "Tell me and I'll forget. Show me and I'll remember. Involve me and I'll learn." Nobody can doubt that she is fulfilling her goal of truly involving her students.

The examples presented here are just a few of the hundreds of interesting e-mail projects going on in English classrooms all over the world. Setting up and implementing such projects may well involve special challenges for teachers, students, and administrators alike, but few who have witnessed the increased motivation and enthusiasm of students in such projects have doubted that the efforts are worthwhile.

As the 21st century approaches, English is becoming the first truly global language. People all over the world—and more nonnative than native speakers—use English daily to do business, conduct research, access academic information, communicate with friends and colleagues, and facilitate cultural exchange.

So often, however, the English that is taught in classrooms is far removed from these authentic and dynamic uses. Advances in electronic communication provide one way to help remedy this problem. It is not the only way, but it is fast, inexpensive, and convenient, thus allowing teachers new and exciting opportunities to help students—whether in a single classroom or across the globe—share information and ideas in English as they never have before.

REFERENCES

Barson, J., Frommer, J., & Schwartz, M. (1993). Foreign language learning using email in a task-oriented perspective: Interuniversity experiments in communication and collaboration. *Journal of Science Education and Technology, 4,* 565–584.

Batson, T. (1988). The ENFI project: A networked classroom approach to writing instruction. *Academic Computing, 2*(5), 32–33.

DiMatteo, A. (1990). Under erasure: A theory for interactive writing in real time. *Computers and Composition, 7*[Special issue], 71–84.

DiMatteo, A. (1991). Communication, writing, learning: An anti-instrumentalist view of network writing. *Computers and Composition, 8*(3), 5–19.

Faigley, L. (1990). Subverting the electronic workbook: Teaching writing using networked computers. In D. Baker & M. Monenberg (Eds.), *The writing teacher as researcher: Essays in the theory and practice of class-based research* (pp. 290-311). Portsmouth, NH: Heinemann.

Janangelo, J. (1991). Technopower and technoppression: Some abuses of power and control in computer-assisted writing environments. *Computers and Composition, 9*(1), 47–63.

Kroonenberg, N. (1994/1995). Developing communicative and thinking skills via electronic mail. *TESOL Journal, 4*(2), 24–27.

Paramskas, D. (1993). Computer-assisted language learning (CALL): Increasingly into an ever more electronic world. *Canadian Modern Language Review, 50,* 124–143.

Robb, T., & Tillyer, A. (1994, November 22). *Penpal advice.* TESL-L Archives [on-line discussion list]. Available e-mail: listserv@cunyvm.cuny.edu

Sayers, D. (1993). Distance team teaching and computer learning networks. *TESOL Journal, 3*(1), 19–23.

Soh, B. L., & Soon, Y. P. (1991). English by e-mail: Creating a global classroom via the medium of computer technology. *ELT Journal, 45,* 287–292.

Susser, B. (1993). Networks and project work: Alternative pedagogies for writing with computers. *Computers and Composition, 10*(3), 63–89.

Warschauer, M., Turbee, L., & Roberts, B. (1994, December). *Computer learning networks and student empowerment* (Research Note 10). Honolulu: University of Hawai'i, Second Language Teaching and Curriculum Center.

Appendix A   Bibliography

Harley, H., & Stout, R. (1994). *The Internet complete reference.* Berkeley, CA: Osborne McGraw-Hill.

Harley, H., & Stout, R. (1994). *The Internet yellow pages.* Berkeley, CA: Osborne McGraw-Hill.

Krol, E. (1994). *The whole Internet.* Sebastopol, CA: O'Reilly.

LaQuey, T. (1993). *The Internet companion.* Reading, MA: Addison-Wesley.

Levine, J., & Baroudi, C. (1993). *The Internet for dummies.* San Mateo, CA: IDG Books.

Wired Magazine. (1994). *Internet unleashed: Everything you need to master the Internet.* Indianapolis: SAMs.

THE INTERNET

Berge, Z., & Collins, M. (1995). *Computer-mediated communication and the online classroom* (Vols. 1–3). Cresskill, NJ: Hampton Press.

Bump, J. (1990). Radical changes in class discussion using networked computers. *Computers and the Humanities, 24,* 49–65.

Cummins, J., & Sayers, D. (1995). *Brave new schools: Challenging cultural illiteracy through global learning networks.* New York: St. Martin's Press.

Dubrovsky, V., Kiesler, S., & Sethna, B. (1991). The equalization phenomenon: Status effects in computer-mediated and face-to-face decision-making groups. *Human-Computer Interaction, 6,* 119–146.

COMPUTER-MEDIATED COMMUNICATION: GENERAL

Ferrara, K., Brunner, H., & Whittemore, G. (1991). Interactive written discourse as an emergent register. *Written Communication, 8,* 9–33.

Finholt, T., Kiesler, S., & Sproull, L. (1986). *An electronic classroom* (Working Paper). Pittsburgh, PA: Carnegie-Mellon University.

Garrison, D. R., & Baynton, M. (1987). Beyond independence in distance education: The concept of control. *American Journal of Distance Education, 1*(3), 3–15.

Harasim, L. (1986). Computer learning networks: Educational applications of computer conferencing. *Journal of Distance Education, 1*(1).

Harasim, L. (Ed.). (1990). *Online education: Perspectives on a new environment.* New York: Praeger.

Hartman, K., Neuwirth, C., Kiesler, S., Sproull, L., Cochran, C., Palmquist, M., & Zubrow, D. (1991). Patterns of social interaction and learning to write: Some effects of networked technologies. *Written Communication, 8,* 79–113.

Hawisher, G., & LeBlanc, P. (1992). *Re-imagining computers and composition: Teaching and research in the virtual age.* Portsmouth, NH: Heinemann.

Hiltz, S. R. (1990, June). Collaborative learning: The virtual classroom approach. *T.H.E. Journal,* 59–65.

Hiltz, S. R. (1992). Constructing and evaluating the virtual classroom. In M. Lea (Ed.), *Contexts of computer-mediated communication.* New York: Harvester Wheatsheaf.

Hiltz, S. R., & Turoff, M. (1993). *The network nation: Human communication via computer.* Cambridge, MA: MIT Press.

Huff, C., & King, R. (1988, August). An experiment in electronic collaboration. In J. D. Goodchilds (Ed.), *Interacting by computer: Effects on small group style and structure.* Symposium conducted at the meeting of the American Psychological Association, Atlanta, GA.

McComb, M. (1993). Augmenting a group discussion course with computer-mediated communication in a small college setting. *Interpersonal Computing and Technology, 1*(3), n.p.

McGuire, T., Kiesler, S., & Siegel, J. (1987). Group and computer-mediated discussion effects in risk decision making. *Journal of Personality and Social Psychology, 52,* 917–930.

Murray, D. (1988). Computer-mediated communication: Implications for ESP. *English for Specific Purposes, 7,* 3–18.

Murray, D. (1991). The composing process for computer conversation. *Written Communication, 8,* 35–55.

Murray, D. (1991). *Conversation for action: The computer terminal as medium of communication.* Philadelphia: J. Benjamins.

Phillips, G., Santoro, G., & Kuehn, S. (1988). The use of computer-mediated communication in training students in group problem-solving and decision-making techniques. *American Journal of Distance Education, 2*(1), 38–51.

Reil, M., & Levin, J. (1990). Building electronic communities: Success and failure in computer networking. *Instructional Science, 19,* 145–169.

Siegel, J., Dubrovsky, V., Kiesler, S., & McGuire, T. W. (1986). Group processes in computer-mediated communication. *Organizational Behavior and Human Decisions Processes, 37,* 157–187.

Sproull, L., & Kiesler, S. (1986). Reducing social context clues: Electronic mail in organizational communication. *Management Science, 32,* 1492–1512.

Sproull, L., & Kiesler, S. (1991). *Connections: New ways of working in the networked organization.* Cambridge, MA: MIT Press.

COMPUTER NETWORKING: SECOND AND FOREIGN LANGUAGE TEACHING

Barson, J., Frommer, J., & Schwartz, M. (1993). Foreign language learning using email in a task-oriented perspective: Interuniversity experiments in communication and collaboration. *Journal of Science Education and Technology, 4,* 565–584.

Beauvois, M. H. (1992). Computer-assisted classroom discussion in the foreign language classroom: Conversation in slow motion. *Foreign Language Annals, 25,* 455–464.

Chun, D. (1994). Using computer networking to facilitate the acquisition of interactive competence. *System, 22,* 17–31.

Cohen, M., & Miyake, N. (1986). A worldwide intercultural network: Exploring electronic messaging for instruction. *Instruction Science, 15,* 257–273.

Cummins, J., & Sayers, D. (1990). Education 2001: Learning networks and educational reform. *Computers in the Schools, 7*(1-2), 1–29.

Davis, B. H., & Chang, Y.-L. (1994/1995). Long-distance collaboration with on-line conferencing. *TESOL Journal, 4*(2), 29–31.

Esling, J. (1991). Researching the effects of networking: Evaluating the spoken and written discourse. In P. Dunkel (Ed.), *Computer-assisted language learning and testing: Research issues and practice* (pp. 111-131). New York: Newbury House.

Goodwin, A. A., Hamrick, J., & Stewart, T. (1993). Instructional delivery via electronic mail. *TESOL Journal, 3*(1), 24–27.

Irvine, M. (1994). *Write around the world.* Scandicci, Italy: Reporter. (*mc7386@mclink.it*)

Kelm, O. (1992). The use of synchronous computer networks in second language instruction: A preliminary report. *Foreign Language Annals, 25,* 441–454.

Kern, R. (1993, November). *Restructuring classroom interaction with networked computers: Effects on quantity and characteristics of language production.* Paper presented at the meeting of the American Council of Teachers of Foreign Languages, San Antonio, TX.

Kiesler, S., Zubrow, D., & Moses, A. M. (1985). Affect in computer-mediated communication: An experiment in synchronous terminal-to-terminal discussion. *Human-Computer Interaction, 1,* 77–104.

Kroonenberg, N. (1994/1995). Developing communicative and thinking skills via electronic mail. *TESOL Journal, 4*(2), 24–27.

Paramskas, D. (1993). Computer-assisted language learning (CALL): Increasingly into an ever more electronic world. *Canadian Modern Language Review, 50,* 124–143.

Payne, J. (1993). The last entry was love: Writing a play on a network. *TESOL Journal, 3*(1), 40.

Pratt, E., & Sullivan, N. (1994, March). *Comparison of ESL writers in networked and regular classrooms.* Paper presented at the 28th Annual TESOL Convention, Baltimore, MD.

Sayers, D. (1993). Distance team teaching and computer learning networks. *TESOL Journal, 3*(1), 19–23.

Soh, B. L., & Soon, Y. P. (1991). English by e-mail: Creating a global classroom via the medium of computer technology. *ELT Journal, 45,* 287–292.

Sullivan, N. (1993). Teaching writing on a computer network. *TESOL Journal, 3*(1), 34–35.

Tella, S. (1991). *Introducing international communications networks and electronic mail into foreign language classrooms* (Research Report No. 95). Helsinki: University of Helsinki, Department of Teacher Education.

Tella, S. (1992a). *Boys, girls and e-mail: A case study in Finnish senior secondary schools* (Research Report No. 110). Helsinki: University of Helsinki, Department of Teacher Education.

Tella, S. (1992b). *Talking shop via e-mail: A thematic and linguistic analysis of electronic mail communication.* (Research Report No. 99). Helsinki: University of Helsinki, Department of Teacher Education.

Tillyer, D. (1993). World peace and natural writing through email. *Collegiate Microcomputer, 11*(2), 67–69.

Wang, Y. M. (1993). *Email dialogue journaling in an ESL reading and writing classroom.* Unpublished doctoral dissertation, University of Oregon at Eugene.

Warschauer, M. (Ed.). (in press). *Virtual connections: Online activities and projects for networking language learners.* Honolulu: University of Hawai'i, Second Language Teaching and Curriculum Center. (for ordering information, e-mail to *nflrc@uhunix.uhcc.hawaii.edu*)

Warschauer, M., Turbee, L., & Roberts, B. (1994, December). *Computer learning networks and student empowerment* (Research Note 10). Honolulu: University of Hawai'i, Second Language Teaching and Curriculum Center.

Bruce, B., Peyton, J. K., & Batson, T. (1993). *Networked-based classrooms: Promises and realities.* Cambridge, England: Cambridge University Press.

Barker, T., & Kemp, F. (1990). Network theory: A postmodern pedagogy for the written classroom. In C. Handa (Ed.), *Computers and community: Teaching composition in the twenty-first century* (pp. 1–27). Portsmouth, NH: Boynton/Cook.

Batson, T. (1988). The ENFI project: A networked classroom approach to writing instruction. *Academic Computing, 2*(5), 32–33.

Batson, T. (1993). Historical barriers to intelligent classroom design. In L. Myers (Ed.), *Approaches to computer writing classrooms: Learning*

COMPUTER NETWORKING: TEACHING ENGLISH (L1) COMPOSITION

from practical experience (pp. 1-34). Albany: State University of New York Press.

Boiarsky, C. (1990). Computers in the classroom: The instruction, the mess, the noise, the writing. In C. Handa (Ed.), *Computers and community: Teaching composition in the twenty-first century* (pp. 47–67). Portsmouth, NH: Boynton/Cook.

Bruce, B., Peyton, J. K., & Batson, T. (Eds.). (1993). *Networked-based classrooms: Promises and realities.* Cambridge, England: Cambridge University Press.

Cooper, M., & Selfe, C. (1990). Computer conferences and learning: Authority, resistance, and internally persuasive discourse. *College English, 52,* 847–869.

DiMatteo, A. (1990). Under erasure: A theory for interactive writing in real time. *Computers and Composition, 7*[Special issue], 71–84.

DiMatteo, A. (1991). Communication, writing, learning: An anti-instrumentalist view of network writing. *Computers and Composition, 8*(3), 5–19.

Eldred, J. (1991). Pedagogy in the computer-networked classroom. *Computers and Composition, 8*(2), 47–61.

Faigley, L. (1990). Subverting the electronic workbook: Teaching writing using networked computers. In D. Baker & M. Monenberg (Eds.), *The writing teacher as researcher: Essays in the theory and practice of class-based research* (pp. 290–311). Portsmouth, NH: Heinemann.

Flores, M. (1990). Computer conferencing: Composing a feminist community of writers. In C. Handa (Ed.), *Computers and community: Teaching composition in the twenty-first century* (pp. 107-139). Portsmouth, NH: Boynton/Cook.

Fox, T. (1990). *The social uses of writing: Politics and pedagogy.* Norwood, NJ: Ablex.

Handa, C. (Ed.). (1990). *Computers and community: Teaching composition in the twenty-first century.* Portsmouth, NH: Boynton/Cook.

Hawisher, G., & Moran, C. (1993). Electronic mail and the writing instructor. *College English, 55,* 627–643.

Hawisher, G., & Selfe, C. (1991). The rhetoric of technology and the electronic writing class. *College Composition and Communication, 42,* 55–65.

Janangelo, J. (1991). Technopower and technoppression: Some abuses of power and control in computer-assisted writing environments. *Computers and Composition, 9,* 47–63.

Kinkead, J. (1987). Computer conversations: E-mail and writing instruction. *College Composition and Communication, 38,* 337–341.

Langston, M. D., & Batson, T. (1990). The social shirts invited by working collaboratively on computer networks: The ENFI project. In C. Handa (Ed.), *Computers and community: Teaching composition in the twenty-first century* (pp. 149–159). Portsmouth, NH: Boynton/Cook.

Mabrito, M. (1991). Electronic mail as a vehicle for peer response: Conversations of high- and low-apprehensive writers. *Written Communication, 8,* 509–532.

Mabrito, M. (1992, December). Computer-mediated communication and high-apprehensive writers: Rethinking the collaborative process. *The Bulletin,* 26–30.

Marx, M. (1990). Distant writers, distant critics, and close readings: Linking composition classes through a peer-critiquing network. *Computers and Composition, 8*(1), 23–29.

Moran, C. (1991). We write, but do we read? *Computers and Composition, 8*(3), 51–61.

Selfe, C. (1990). Technology in the English classroom: Computers through the lens of feminist theory. In C. Handa (Ed.), *Computers and community: Teaching composition in the twenty-first century* (pp. 118–139). Portsmouth, NH: Boynton/Cook.

Selfe, C., & Meyer, P. (1991). Testing claims for on-line conferences. *Written Communications, 8,* 163–192.

Susser, B. (1993). Networks and project work: Alternative pedagogies for writing with computers. *Computers and Composition, 10*(3), 63–89.

CAELL Journal: a paper journal on computer-assisted English language learning. For subscription information, contact *ISTE@oregon.uoregon.edu*.

CALICO Journal: a paper journal covering a range of issues related to computer-assisted language learning. For subscription information, contact *CALICO@acpub.duke.edu*.

Computers and Composition: a paper journal discussing the uses of computers in teaching writing. Available for $15 per year from Departemtn of Humanities, Michigan Technological University, Houghton, MI 49931; telephone (906) 487-2447.

Interpersonal Communications & Technology (IPCT): an electronic journal discussing a wide range of topics related to electronic communication in education and other fields. To receive a free subscription, send the message *subscribe IPCT-J yourfirstname yourlastname* to *listserv@guvm.george-town.edu* or *listserv@guvm.bitnet*.

The Online Educator: a journal, published in both paper and electronic forms, discussing ways to use e-mail and the Internet in education. Sample copies are available for $2 from The Online Educator, Box 251141, West Bloomfield, MI 48325.

   TESL-EJ: An electronic journal on the theory and practice of ESL/EFL teaching. Subscriptions are available free by sending the message *sub TESLEJ-L yourfirstname yourlastname* to *listserv@cmsa.berkeley.edu.*

Contacts and Organizations

Consortium for School Networking: a membership organization of institutions formed to further the development and use of computer network technology in K–12 education. For information, send an e-mail to *ferdi@digital.cosn.org.*

EDNET: a list discussing computer networking and its relationship to education. To subscribe, send the message *subscribe EDNET yourfirstname yourlastname* to *listserv@nic.umass.edu*

EDUTEL: a list discussing computer-mediated communications (CMC) applications in educational contexts. To subscribe, send the message *subscribe EDUTEL yourfirstname yourlastname* to *listserv@rpitsvm.bitnet*

Email Project: an ongoing project linking university students around the world on concrete, challenging research projects. For information, contact Ruth Vilmi at *project@hut.fi*

Global SchoolNet Foundation: a major source of information and resources about linking K–12 students electronically. For information, contact *fred@acme.fred.org*

INCLASS: an e-mail discussion list based in Canada dealing with classroom uses of the Internet. To subscribe, send the message *subscribe inclass yourfirstname yourlastname* to *listproc@schoolnet.carleton.ca*

Intercultural E-Mail Classroom Connections (IECC): together with the three TESL-L lists (below), a great source for finding partner classrooms. It includes four separate lists for (a) finding partners classrooms, (b) announcing projects, (c) discussing general issues related to classroom connections, and (d) making electronic connections at the higher education level. To subscribe and get information about four lists, send the message *subscribe* to *iecc-request@stolaf.edu*

International Education and Resource Network (I*EARN): brings together more than 500 elementary and secondary schools in some 20 countries for a variety of joint projects including shared student publications, exchanges, and comparative investigations. For information, contact *iearn@igc.apc.org*

International Society for Technology in Education: Publishes *CAELL Journal* (see Appendix B), organizes conferences, and offers graduate-level distance education courses. For information, contact *iste@oregon.uoregon.edu*, or check the information directly via Gopher (*iste-gopher.uoregon.edu*).

K12NET: A loosely organized, decentralized network of school-based electronic bulletin board systems throughout North America, Australia, Europe, and the former Soviet Union. For information, contact Jack Crawford, *jack@k12.net.org*

KIDSPHERE: Formed to provide a global network for the use of children and teachers in Grades K–12. It is intended to provide a focus for technological development and for resolving the problems of language, standards, and other issues that inevitably arise in international communications. For further information, send the message *subscribe* to *kidsphere@vms.cis.pitt.edu*

The Online Writery: Based at the University of Missouri, this service has a staff of 10 cybertutors who offer writing instruction via the Internet. For information, contact *writing@showme.missouri.edu*

Purdue University Online Writing Lab (OWL): An on-line center that provides tutoring by e-mail and dozens of helpful documents. For information, send a blank e-mail message to *owl@sage.cc.purdue.edu* (with the subject *owl-request*).

schMOOze University: a special MOO set up for ESL/EFL teachers. For infomration, telnet to *arthur.rutgers.edu 8888*. Further information is also available on the World Wide Web at *http://arthur.rutgers.edu.8888*

Student Lists (SLs): A set of nine e-mail discussion lists for college- and university-level students of ESL/EFL all over the world. For information, send a blank message to *announce-sl@latrobe.edu.au*

TESL-L: An international e-mail discussion list for ESL teachers; one of the largest and most active e-mail lists in the world. Send the message *sub TESL-L yourfirstname yourlastname* to *listserv@cunyvm.cuny.edu* or *listserv@cunyvm.bitnet*

TESLCA-L: A special branch of TESL-L devoted to computer-assisted language learning. For information, you must first join TESL-L (see above) and then send the message *sub TESLCA-L yourfirstname yourlastname* to *listserv@cunyvm.cuny.edu* or *listserv@cunyvm.bitnet*

TESLK-12: A sister list of TESL-L, especially for K–12 teachers. To subscribe, send the message *sub TESLK-12 yourfirstname yourlastname* to *listserv@cunyvm.cuny.edu* or *listserv@cunyvm.cuny.edu*

Appendix D

Glossary

Anonymous FTP: Anonymous File Transfer Protocol; a system for sending or receiving files from a remote computer available to the general public, without any special userid required.

Archie: a system for locating files that are available to the public by Anonymous FTP.

ASCII: American Standard Code for Information Interchange; pure text without any formatting or graphics.

asynchronous: communication that is not instantaneous. Asynchronous messages take anywhere from several seconds to several minutes (or sometimes several hours) to arrive. Asynchronous messages can be read at any time; the recipient need not be logged on at the time of delivery.

baud: when transmitting data, the number of times the medium's state changes per second. For example, a 14,400-baud modem changes the signal it sends in the telephone line 14,400 times per second.

baud rate: the speed of a modem. A 28,800-baud modem is twice as fast as a 14,400-baud modem. See *baud, bps.*

BBS: bulletin board system; allows for posting and reading of messages on a local network; sometimes also connected to the Internet.

bcc: blind carbon copy (or blind courtesy copy); sending a copy of a message to someone without notifying the addressee.

binary file: a file that includes some kind of formatting, graphics, special code, sounds, photos, or video in addition to text.

BITNET: a worldwide computer network that connects over 1,000 academic and research institutes around the world. It is separate from the Internet but connected to it.

body: the main part of an e-mail, where you write your own message (distinguished from the header).

bps: bits per second; the speed at which bits are transmitted over a communications medium. Used synonymously with *baud rate* to refer to the speed of a modem.

browser: a special program used for browsing through and accessing information on the World Wide Web. Popular browsers include Mosaic, Netscape, WebNet, and Lynx.

BTW: by the way; common abbreviation used in e-mail.

CACD: computer-assisted class discussion, also referred to as *ENFI*, *electronic discussion*, or *computer conferencing*.

cc: carbon copy (or courtesy copy).

CELIA: Computer-Enhanced Language Instruction Archive; an archive of computer-assisted language learning software accessible by Gopher and by Anonymous FTP.

client: a software application that extracts some service from a server somewhere on the network on your behalf. For example, Tiny Fugue is a client that provides a special interface for working with MOO servers.

computer-mediated communication (CMC): the use of one or more computers to mediate or facilitate communication between two or more people.

cyberspace: an amorphous term used to refer to the world of electronic communication.

cybersurfing: using various tools to search for information on the Internet. Also referred to as *surfing the Net*.

Daedalus InterChange: a popular program for real-time communication in the composition and language classroom.

domain: the second part of an e-mail address, following the @ sign (for example, *whitehouse.gov* in *president@whitehouse.gov*), indicating the particular computer that is hooked up to the Internet.

download: to copy computer files in a direction closer to you (e.g., from a remote computer to your Internet directory or from your

Internet directory to your personal computer).

Elm: a popular program for sending e-mail.

e-mail: electronic mail; a way of sending messages asynchronously between two or more individuals both connected via computer. Also spelled *E-mail* and *email*.

emoticon: a symbol used to convey emotion on e-mail, for example, :-) (a smile) or :-((a frown); also referred to as a *smiley*.

ENFI: electronic networking for interaction, a term for classroom electronic discussion that was coined and copyrighted by Gallaudet University.

FAQ: a frequently asked question, or, more commonly, a list of frequently asked questions pertaining to the use of a particular USENET newsgroup or e-mail discussion list.

flame: to use unnecessarily hostile language in e-mail or on a newsgroup.

FTP: File Transfer Protocol, an application program for passing files from one computer to another.

FYI: for your information; an abbreviation commonly used in e-mail.

Gopher: a menu-based system for exploring resources on the Internet.

header: the top part of an e-mail, which includes at least *to, from, date*, and *subject* (as distinguished from the body).

hypertext: a nonlinear, multilayered system of information in which files (of texts, and often graphics or audiovisual elements) are linked to each other and are accessed by pointing to or choosing particular references. Also called *hypermedia*.

HTML: hypertext markup language; a language used for telling a World Wide Web browser how to lay out text (and other media) and how to make links to other parts or documents.

HTTP: hypertext transfer protocol; the protocol on which the World Wide Web is based.

IMHO: in my humble opinion, an abbreviation frequently used in e-mail.

InterChange: See Daedalus Interchange.

Internet: the largest worldwide network of computer networks, providing electronic mail, newsgroups, file transfer, and other services.

IP: Internet protocol; the protocol that allows a packet of data to traverse multiple networks on its way to its final destination.

keypals: computer pen pals.

LAN: local area network; computers in a single location that are networked together.

LISTSERV: (a) the most widely used software program for e-mail discussion lists; (b) one of the e-mail discussion lists that uses the LISTSERV software; (c) a term often used to refer to e-mail discussion lists in general.

lurk: to read messages on a discussion list or computer conference without participating.

majordomo: after LISTSERV, another software program used for e-mail discussion lists.

modem: a device that connects a computer to a telephone line. An internal modem comes on a card that fits on a slot inside your computer; an external modem is placed outside.

MOO: technically, *MUD, object oriented*. A graphic- and text-based multi-user environment where people from around the world can chat in real time and perform variety of simulations.

MUD: multiuser domain. A text-based computer environment where people can communicate in real time and carry out various types of simulations. For the most part it has been superseded by MOOs, which are similar in character but are graphic based in addition to being text based.

the Net: used to refer to the Internet or sometimes to any computer network, e.g., "See you on the Net."

Netscape: the most popular browser used for accessing information on the World Wide Web.

netiquette: net etiquette; etiquette for polite and appropriate communications on computer networks.

Network News: See USENET.

newsgroup: a discussion group on USENET.

nomail: an option on LISTSERV discussion lists whereby no messages are sent to your mailbox, but you retain list membership and privilege (sending messages, accessing archives).

Pine: a popular and easy-to-use program for sending e-mail.

post: to send a message onto a discussion list or newsgroup.

PPP: point to point protocol, a protocol that allows a computer with modem and telephone line to provide a maximum Internet connection. A newer standard than SLIP.

protocol: a definition for how computers shall act when communicating with each other.

real-time: communication that takes place immediately, with all participants simultaneously logged on to their computers and messages being transferred instantaneously (also called *synchronous*).

schMOOze University: a special MOO for ESL/EFL students and teachers (based in part on a cow motif). See *MOO*.

server: (a) software that allows a computer to offer a service to another computer (The other computers contact the server program by using a matching **client** software.); (b) the computer on which the server software runs.

signature: a short file that people often insert at the end of e-mail messages. It includes the person's name, e-mail address, and perhaps other information such as snail mail address or telephone number. Some e-mail programs allow users to create a signature file and have it automatically inserted in all their messages.

SLIP: serial line Internet protocol; a protocol that allows a computer with modem and telephone line to provide a maximum Internet connection.

snail mail: mail delivered by the postal service.

surfing the Net: using various tools to search for information on the Internet.

synchronous: communication that takes place immediately, with all participants simultaneously logged on to their computers and messages being transferred instantaneously (also called *real-time*).

telnet: an application program that allows you to log on to a remote computer.

TESL-L: An e-mail discussion list for teachers of ESL/EFL.

UNIX: a computer operating system that is used on many of the mainframe computers that help operate the Internet.

upload: to copy computer files in a direction away from you (e.g., from your personal computer into your Internet directory or from your Internet directory to a remote computer).

URL: Uniform Resource Locator; an address system used in the World Wide Web for finding resources throughout the Internet.

USENET: an informal collection of more than 5,000 newsgroups that exchange news and information. Sometimes called *Network News*.

userid: user identification; the name or nickname a person chooses for a login and e-mail address. The userid is the part of the e-mail address before the @ sign; for example, *president* in *president@whitehouse.gov*.

Veronica: a system for finding files in Gophers around the world.

WAIS: wide area information servers; a powerful system for looking up information in data bases throughout the Internet.

WAN: wide area network; computers networked together over a broad geographical area.

World Wide Web: an all-in-one, hypertext-based system for accessing various resources on the Internet. Also referred to as *WWW* or *the Web*.

Also available from TESOL

All Things to All People
Donald C. Flemming, Lucie C. Germer, and Christiane Kelley

A New Decade of Language Testing Research:
Selected Papers From the 1990 Language Testing Research Colloquium
Dan Douglas and Carol Chapelle, Editors

Books for a Small Planet:
An Intercultural Bibliography for Young English Language Learners
Dorothy S. Brown

Common Threads of Practice:
Teaching English to Children Around the World
Katharine Davies Samway and Denise McKeon, Editors

Dialogue Journal Writing with Nonnative English Speakers:
A Handbook for Teachers
Joy Kreeft Peyton and Leslee Reed

Dialogue Journal Writing with Nonnative English Speakers:
An Instructional Packet for Teachers and Workshop Leaders
Joy Kreeft Peyton and Jana Staton

Discourse and Performance of International Teaching Assistants
Carolyn G. Madden and Cynthia L. Myers, Editors

Diversity as Resource:
Redefining Cultural Literacy
Denise E. Murray, Editor

New Ways in Teacher Education
Donald Freeman, with Steve Cornwell, Editors